# ❖❖studysync®

## Reading & Writing Companion

## Test of Time

Why do we still read myths and folktales?

## studysync

**studysync.com**

Send all inquiries to:
BookheadEd Learning, LLC
610 Daniel Young Drive
Sonoma, CA  95476

ISBN 978-1-94-469583-5

7 8 9 B&B 24 23 22
C

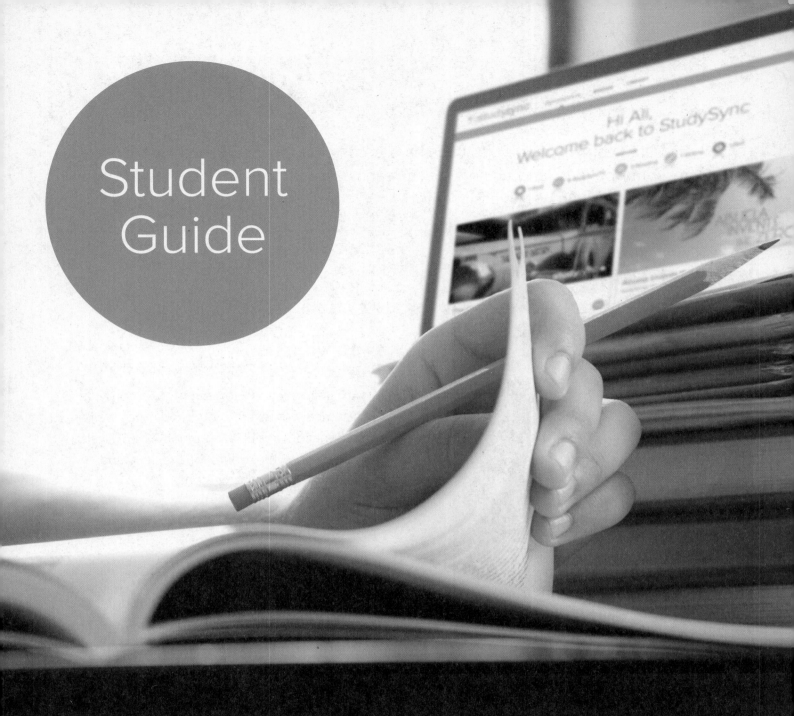

# Student Guide

## Getting Started

**W**elcome to the StudySync Reading & Writing Companion! In this book, you will find a collection of readings based on the theme of the unit you are studying. As you work through the readings, you will be asked to answer questions and perform a variety of tasks designed to help you closely analyze and understand each text selection. Read on for an explanation of each

# Close Reading and Writing Routine

In each unit, you will read texts that share a common theme, despite their different genres, time periods, and authors. Each reading encourages a closer look through questions and a short writing assignment.

Rikki-Tikki-Tavi

FICTION
Rudyard Kipling
1894

## Introduction

**studysync**

"Rikki-Tikki-Tavi" is one of the most famous tales from *The Jungle Book*, a collection of short stories published in 1894 by English author Rudyard Kipling (1865–1936). The stories in *The Jungle Book* feature animal characters with anthropomorphic traits and are intended to be read as fables, each illustrating a moral lesson. In this story, Rikki-tikki-tavi is a courageous young mongoose adopted as a pet by a British family living in 19th-century colonial India.

"Rikki-tikki held on with his eyes shut, for now he was quite sure he was dead."

This is the story of the great war that Rikki-tikki-tavi fought single-handed, through the bath-rooms of the big bungalow in Segowlee cantonment. Darzee, the Tailorbird, helped him, and Chuchundra, the musk-rat, who never comes out into the middle of the floor, but always creeps round by the wall, gave him advice, but Rikki-tikki did the real fighting.

He was a mongoose, rather like a little cat in his fur and his tail, but quite like a weasel in his head and his habits. His eyes and the end of his restless nose were pink. He could scratch himself anywhere he pleased with any leg, front or back, that he chose to use. He could fluff up his tail till it looked like a bottle brush, and his war cry as he scuttled through the long grass was: "Rikk-tikk-tikki-tikki-tchk!"

One day, a high summer flood washed him out of the burrow where he lived with his father and mother, and carried him, kicking and clucking, down a roadside ditch. He found a little wisp of grass floating there, and clung to it till he lost his senses. When he revived, he was lying in the hot sun on the middle of a garden path, very draggled indeed, and a small boy was saying, "Here's a dead mongoose. Let's have a funeral!"

"No," said his mother, "let's take him in and dry him. Perhaps he isn't really dead."

They took him into the house, and a big man picked him up between his finger and thumb and said he was not dead but half choked. So they wrapped him in cotton wool, and warmed him over a little fire, and he opened his eyes and sneezed.

"Now," said the big man (he was an Englishman who had just moved into the bungalow), "don't frighten him, and we'll see what he'll do."

 **Skill:** Textual Evidence

It says that he fluffs up his tail and he has a war cry. I know that a war cry is used in battle to rally the troops. This must mean that Rikki-tikki is brave and powerful, like a soldier.

**Skill:** Text-Dependent Responses

After finding Rikki-tikki, the English family brought him into their home and took care of him.

## ① Introduction

An Introduction to each text provides historical context for your reading as well as information about the author. You will also learn about the genre of the text and the year in which it was written.

## ② Notes

Many times, while working through the activities after each text, you will be asked to **annotate** or **make annotations** about what you are reading. This means that you should highlight or underline words in the text and use the "Notes" column to make comments or jot down any questions you have. You may also want to note any unfamiliar vocabulary words here.

You will also see sample student annotations to go along with the Skill lesson for that text.

## 3  First Read

During your first reading of each selection, you should just try to get a general idea of the content and message of the reading. Don't worry if there are parts you don't understand or words that are unfamiliar to you. You'll have an opportunity later to dive deeper into the text.

## 4  Think Questions

These questions will ask you to start thinking critically about the text, asking specific questions about its purpose, and making connections to your prior knowledge and reading experiences. To answer these questions, you should go back to the text and draw upon specific evidence to support your responses. You will also begin to explore some of the more challenging vocabulary words in the selection.

## 5  Skills

Each Skill includes two parts: Checklist and Your Turn. In the Checklist, you will learn the process for analyzing the text. The model student annotations in the text provide examples of how you might make your own notes following the instructions in the Checklist. In the Your Turn, you will use those same instructions to practice the skill.

---

### 3

First Read

Read "Rikki-Tikki-Tavi." After you read, complete the Think Questions below.

### 4  ☁ THINK QUESTIONS

1. How did Rikki-tikki come to live with the English family? Cite specific evidence from the text to support your answer.

2. What do the descriptions of Nag and the dialogue in paragraphs 23–24 suggest about Nag's character? Cite specific evidence from the text to support your answer.

3. Describe in two to three sentences how Rikki-tikki saves the family from snakes.

4. Find the word **cultivated** in paragraph 18 of "Rikki-Tikki-Tavi." Use context clues in the surrounding sentences, as well as the sentence in which the word appears, to determine the word's meaning. Write your definition here and identify clues that helped you figure out the word's meaning.

5. Use context clues to determine the meaning of **sensible** as it is used in paragraph 79 of "Rikki-Tikki-Tavi." Write your definition of *sensible* here and identify clues that helped you figure out the meaning. Then check the meaning in the dictionary.

---

### 5

Skill:
Character

Use the Checklist to analyze Character in "Rikki-Tikki-Tavi." Refer to the sample student annotations about Character in the text.

#### ••• CHECKLIST FOR CHARACTER

In order to determine how particular elements of a story or drama interact, note the following:

✓ the characters in the story, including the protagonist and antagonist

✓ the settings and how they shape the characters or plot

✓ plot events and how they affect the characters

✓ key events or series of episodes in the plot, especially events that cause characters to react, respond, or change in some way

✓ characters' responses as the plot reaches a climax and moves toward a resolution of the problem facing the protagonist

✓ the resolution of the conflict in the plot and the ways that affects each character

To analyze how particular elements of a story or drama interact, consider the following questions:

✓ How do the characters' responses change or develop from the beginning to the end of the story?

✓ How does the setting shape the characters and plot in the story?

✓ How do the events in the plot affect the characters? How do they develop as a result of the conflict, climax, and resolution?

✓ Do the characters' problems reach a resolution? How?

#### ⟳ YOUR TURN

1. How does the mother's love for her son affect her actions in paragraph 37?

   ○ A. It prompts her to keep her son away from Rikki-tikki.
   ○ B. It causes a disagreement between her and her husband.
   ○ C. It makes her show affection towards Rikki-tikki.
   ○ D. It makes Rikki-tikki feel nervous staying with the family.

2. What does the dialogue in paragraph 40 suggest about Chuchundra?

   ○ A. He is afraid.
   ○ B. He is easily fooled.
   ○ C. He is optimistic.
   ○ D. He loves Rikki-tikki.

3. Which paragraph shows that Teddy looks to Rikki-tikki for protection?

   ○ A. 37
   ○ B. 38
   ○ C. 39
   ○ D. 40

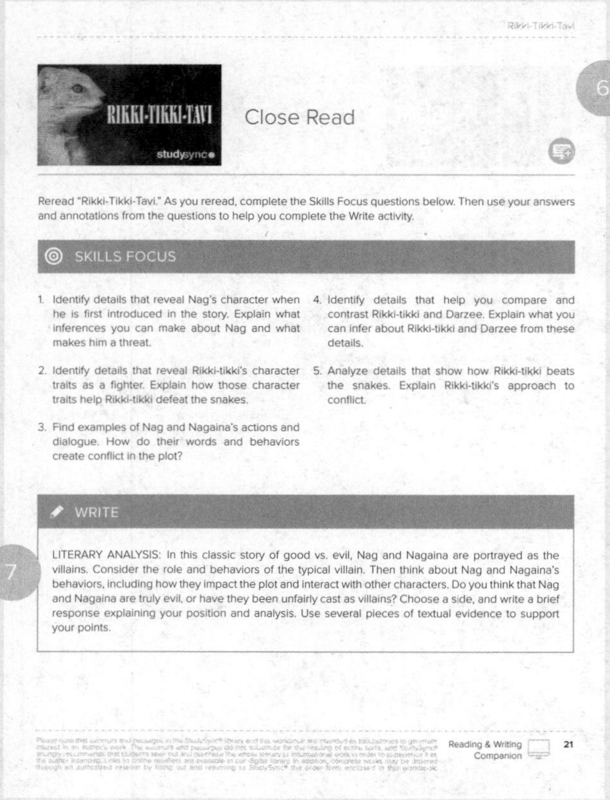

Rikki-Tikki-Tavi

RIKKI-TIKKI-TAVI studysync

Close Read

Reread "Rikki-Tikki-Tavi." As you reread, complete the Skills Focus questions below. Then use your answers and annotations from the questions to help you complete the Write activity.

SKILLS FOCUS

1. Identify details that reveal Nag's character when he is first introduced in the story. Explain what inferences you can make about Nag and what makes him a threat.
2. Identify details that reveal Rikki-tikki's character traits as a fighter. Explain how those character traits help Rikki-tikki defeat the snakes.
3. Find examples of Nag and Nagaina's actions and dialogue. How do their words and behaviors create conflict in the plot?
4. Identify details that help you compare and contrast Rikki-tikki and Darzee. Explain what you can infer about Rikki-tikki and Darzee from these details.
5. Analyze details that show how Rikki-tikki beats the snakes. Explain Rikki-tikki's approach to conflict.

WRITE

LITERARY ANALYSIS: In this classic story of good vs. evil, Nag and Nagaina are portrayed as the villains. Consider the role and behaviors of the typical villain. Then think about Nag and Nagaina's behaviors, including how they impact the plot and interact with other characters. Do you think that Nag and Nagaina are truly evil, or have they been unfairly cast as villains? Choose a side, and write a brief response explaining your position and analysis. Use several pieces of textual evidence to support your points.

Reading & Writing Companion 21

Ready for Marcos

FICTION

Introduction

Twelve-year-old Monica Alvarez has a happy life. She is a star on the track team and has many good friends. But everything changes when her parents bring Marcos, her new baby brother, home from the hospital. Her parents want her to have more responsibilities. Monica wonders what it will mean to be a big sister. Is she ready? Is she willing?

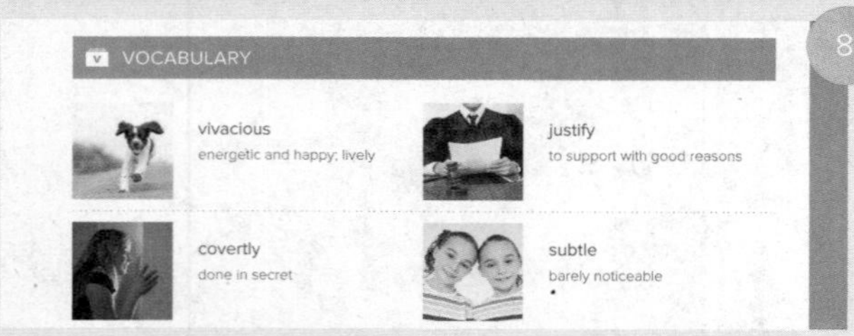

VOCABULARY

vivacious
energetic and happy; lively

justify
to support with good reasons

covertly
done in secret

subtle
barely noticeable

## 6 Close Read & Skills Focus

After you have completed the First Read, you will be asked to go back and read the text more closely and critically. Before you begin your Close Read, you should read through the Skills Focus to get an idea of the concepts you will want to focus on during your second reading. You should work through the Skills Focus by making annotations, highlighting important concepts, and writing notes or questions in the "Notes" column. Depending on instructions from your teacher, you may need to respond online or use a separate piece of paper to start expanding on your thoughts and ideas.

## 7 Write

Your study of each selection will end with a writing assignment. For this assignment, you should use your notes, annotations, personal ideas, and answers to both the Think and Skills Focus questions. Be sure to read the prompt carefully and address each part of it in your writing.

## 8 English Language Learner

The English Language Learner texts focus on improving language proficiency. You will practice learning strategies and skills in individual and group activities to become better readers, writers, and speakers.

# Extended Writing Project and Grammar

This is your opportunity to use genre characteristics and craft to compose meaningful, longer written works exploring the theme of each unit. You will draw information from your readings, research, and own life experiences to complete the assignment.

## 1 Writing Project

After you have read all of the unit text selections, you will move on to a writing project. Each project will guide you through the process of writing your essay. Student models will provide guidance and help you organize your thoughts. One unit ends with an **Extended Oral Project,** which will give you an opportunity to develop your oral language and communication skills.

## 2 Writing Process Steps

There are four steps in the writing process: Plan, Draft, Revise, and Edit and Publish. During each step, you will form and shape your writing project, and each lesson's peer review will give you the chance to receive feedback from your peers and teacher.

## 3 Writing Skills

Each Skill lesson focuses on a specific strategy or technique that you will use during your writing project. Each lesson presents a process for applying the skill to your own work and gives you the opportunity to practice it to improve your writing.

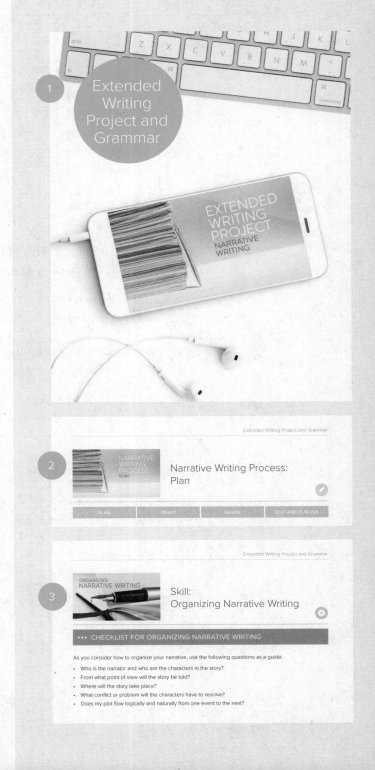

Reading & Writing Companion

**vii**

# Test of Time

Why do we still read myths and folktales?

Genre Focus: FICTION—MYTHS & FOLKTALES

## Texts

 Paired Readings

# Extended Writing Project and Grammar

# Why do we still read myths and folktales?

### AESOP

The ancient Greek author known as Aesop (c. 620–564 BCE) is believed to have been born on the Black Coast near Nesebar in modern-day Bulgaria. Legend has it that he was enslaved by a man named Xanthus, but was eventually freed, before meeting his demise in Delphi on trumped-up charges that saw him thrown off a cliff. Aesop is best known for his fables, stories passed down by oral tradition that he transcribed, intended to teach political, moral, and ethical lessons to young readers.

### AIMEE BENDER

Aimee Bender (b. 1969) was born in Southern California, and attended the University of California, San Diego, before earning her MFA at the University of California, Irvine. A former director of the University of Southern California's Ph.D. program in Creative Writing and Literature, she has also taught at UCLA and worked on outreach programs that develop literacy for disadvantaged populations. She is the author of seven books, including *The Particular Sadness of Lemon Cake*, *The Color Master*, and *An Invisible Sign of My Own*. She lives in Los Angeles.

### SUZANNE COLLINS

Before penning the *New York Times* best-selling series *The Hunger Games* Trilogy, and seeing her books adapted for the big screen, Suzanne Collins (b. 1962) wrote for the children's television network Nickelodeon. After graduating from Indiana University, she worked as a staff writer for several shows, including *Clarissa Explains It All*, *The Mystery Files of Shelby Woo*, *Little Bear*, and *Oswald*. Not long after, she wrote her first bestselling series, *The Underland Chronicles*. Worldwide, the books she has written have sold over 100 million copies.

### ROBERT HAYDEN

When his parents separated, Robert Hayden (1913–1980) was raised from infancy in a foster home filled with anger and violence in the Detroit neighborhood Paradise Valley, where artists like Billie Holiday and Ella Fitzgerald took to the stage. Because of severe nearsightedness, Hayden chose books over sports, kindling a lifetime love. He attended Detroit City College, and went on to the University of Michigan for graduate studies. Hayden may be best known for his works "The Middle Passage" and "Those Winter Sundays." He died in Ann Arbor.

### EMMA LAZARUS

Born into a wealthy family, Emma Lazarus (1849–1887) grew up in New York City. Shortly after her father published some of her poetry, she was published by a commercial press and caught the eye of Ralph Waldo Emerson, among others. Over the next ten years, she'd publish another collection of poetry, *Admetus and Other Poems*; a novel, *Alide: An Episode in Goethe's Life*; and a play, *The Spagnoletto*. However, she is best known for her sonnet on the pedestal of the Statue of Liberty, written at the request of fundraisers on behalf of the monument.

## JOSEPHINE PRESTON PEABODY

Born in Brooklyn and raised in Massachusetts after the death of her father, Josephine Preston Peabody (1874–1922) grew up in poverty in the home of her maternal grandmother, reading and writing constantly. She had her first poem published at the age of fourteen. After her other poems were published in the *Atlantic Monthly* and *Scribner's Magazine*, a patron funded her schooling, and Peabody enrolled at Radcliffe College. She'd go on to publish collections of poetry, a one-act play, and several other books, while also lecturing at Wellesley.

## CHARLOTTE BLAKE ALSTON

Charlotte Blake Alston is a storyteller, singer, and narrator who has performed at the Kennedy Center, Lincoln Center, and abroad from Cape Town, South Africa, to a refugee camp in northern Senegal. Her focus is on African and African American stories, and her solo performances often include accompaniment by traditional instruments, including djembe, kalimba, and the twenty-one-stringed kora. For over two decades she has served as the host for family and school concerts at the Philadelphia Orchestra and at Carnegie Hall.

## FARAH AHMEDI

At the age of ten, Afghanistan-born author Farah Ahmedi (b. 1987) was severely injured when she stepped on a landmine. Ahmedi was hospitalized in Germany where she underwent a leg amputation. Upon her return to Afghanistan, Ahmedi's father and sisters were killed in a rocket attack, and her brothers disappeared fleeing the Taliban. She moved to the United States after gaining refugee status, where she won *Good Morning America*'s Story of My Life contest, wrote her memoir, and has become an outspoken humanitarian and advocate for people with disabilities.

## JAMES BALDWIN

An educator and administrator for eighteen years, James Baldwin (1841–1925) served as a school superintendent in Indiana before becoming a textbook editor and prolific children's author of more than fifty books. Baldwin's works, of which it is estimated that 26 million copies were sold worldwide, cover topics ranging from Greek mythology to famous American historical figures.

## M. R. COX

London native and dedicated folklorist Marian Roalfe Cox (1860–1916) began attending meetings of the British Folklore Society with her mother as a young girl. Described as "pale" and "fragile-looking" in her early years, Cox's diligence was soon apparent. In her twenties, she undertook the project of cataloging and categorizing every version of the "Cinderella" fairy tale told around the world. The resulting anthology, published in 1893, became the definitive text on the subject and expanded our understanding of how stories are passed on across the world.

## BARRY STRAUSS

At Cornell University, Barry Strauss (b. 1953) serves as a professor of humanities, history, and the classics. Strauss is a series editor for the Princeton History of the Ancient World series, a military historian, and the author of seven books, including *The Death of Caesar, Masters of Command*, and *The Spartacus War*. A former graduate of Cornell University, he received his BA there before moving on to Yale University for his master's and Ph.D. He also currently serves as the director and founder of Cornell's Program on Freedom and Free Societies.

# Aesop's Fables

FICTION
Aesop
600 BCE

## Introduction

There are facts and fictions surrounding the person known as Aesop. Once an enslaved African who was freed for his wit and intelligence—and reportedly thrown to his death over a precipice by the people of Delphi—Aesop is credited with creating hundreds of fables, though none of his actual writings survive. What can't be disputed is that the short, charming tales of wisdom and folly have left an indelible mark on Western culture. In this selection of seven fables, not all have

# "Pleasure bought with pains, hurts."

### The Swollen Fox

1   A VERY HUNGRY FOX, seeing some bread and meat left by shepherds in the hollow of an oak, crept into the hole and made a hearty meal. When he finished, he was so full that he was not able to get out, and began to groan and lament his fate. Another Fox passing by heard his cries, and coming up, inquired the cause of his complaining. On learning what had happened, he said to him, "Ah, you will have to remain there, my friend, until you become such as you were when you crept in, and then you will easily get out."

### The Flies and the Honey-Pot

2   A NUMBER of Flies were attracted to a jar of honey which had been overturned in a housekeeper's room, and placing their feet in it, ate greedily. Their feet, however, became so smeared with the honey that they could not use their wings, nor release themselves, and were suffocated. Just as they were expiring, they exclaimed, "O foolish creatures that we are, for the sake of a little pleasure we have destroyed ourselves." Pleasure bought with pains, hurts.

### The Hen and the Golden Eggs

3   A COTTAGER[1] and his wife had a Hen that laid a golden egg every day. They supposed that the Hen must contain a great lump of gold in its inside, and in order to get the gold they killed it. Having done so, they found to their surprise that the Hen differed in no respect from their other hens. The foolish pair, thus hoping to become rich all at once, **deprived** themselves of the gain of which they were assured day by day.

### The Miser

4   A **MISER** sold all that he had and bought a lump of gold, which he buried in a hole in the ground by the side of an old wall and went to look at daily. One of his workmen observed his frequent visits to the spot and decided to watch his movements. He soon discovered the secret of the hidden treasure, and digging down, came to the lump of gold, and stole it. The Miser, on his next visit, found the hole empty and began to tear his hair and to make loud

---

1. **cottager**  a person living in a cottage

Skill:
Theme

*Because this is a fable, a lesson will be taught at the end. I think the theme will be related to the lesson. The topic of this fable is about eating. I think the theme might have to do with how eating too much could be a problem.*

Skill:
Theme

*The Fox learns a lesson from another Fox— that he can't get out of the hole until he is hungry again. The Fox's challenge is that he got too big to crawl out! The theme must be that too much of a good thing can lead to trouble.*

lamentations. A neighbor, seeing him overcome with grief and learning the cause, said, "Pray do not grieve so; but go and take a stone, and place it in the hole, and fancy that the gold is still lying there. It will do you quite the same service; for when the gold was there, you had it not, as you did not make the slightest use of it."

### The Fox and the Woodcutter

5    A FOX, running before the hounds, came across a Woodcutter felling an oak and begged him to show him a safe hiding-place. The Woodcutter advised him to take shelter in his own hut, so the Fox crept in and hid himself in a corner. The huntsman[2] soon came up with his hounds and inquired of the Woodcutter if he had seen the Fox. He declared that he had not seen him, and yet pointed, all the time he was speaking, to the hut where the Fox lay hidden. The huntsman took no notice of the signs, but believing his word, hastened forward in the chase. As soon as they were well away, the Fox departed without taking any notice of the Woodcutter: whereon he called to him and reproached him, saying, "You ungrateful fellow, you owe your life to me, and yet you leave me without a word of thanks." The Fox replied, "Indeed, I should have thanked you **fervently** if your deeds had been as good as your words, and if your hands had not been traitors to your speech."

### The Ants and the Grasshopper

6    THE ANTS were spending a fine winter's day drying grain collected in the summertime. A Grasshopper, **perishing** with famine, passed by and earnestly begged for a little food. The Ants inquired of him, "Why did you not treasure up food during the summer?" He replied, "I had not leisure enough. I passed the days in singing." They then said in **derision:** "If you were foolish enough to sing all the summer, you must dance supperless to bed in the winter."

The Ant and the Grasshopper

### The Wolf in Sheep's Clothing

7    ONCE UPON A TIME a Wolf **resolved** to disguise his appearance in order to secure food more easily. Encased in the skin of a sheep, he pastured with the flock deceiving the shepherd by his costume. In the evening he was shut up by the shepherd in the fold; the gate was closed, and the entrance made thoroughly secure. But the shepherd, returning to the fold during the night to obtain meat for the next day, mistakenly caught up the Wolf instead of a sheep, and killed him instantly.

8    Harm seek. Harm find.

---

2. **huntsman** hunter

# First Read

Read "Aesop's Fables." After you read, complete the Think Questions below.

## ☁ THINK QUESTIONS

1. How are the moral lessons in "The Swollen Fox" and "The Flies and the Honey-Pot" alike? Cite textual evidence and explain your answer.

2. How is the Wolf's predicament in "The Wolf in Sheep's Clothing" similar to that of the cottager and his wife in "The Hen and the Golden Eggs"? Cite textual evidence as you compare the two tales.

3. How are the cottager and his wife in "The Hen and the Golden Eggs" similar to the Miser in "The Miser"? What lesson is Aesop teaching in both fables? Cite passages in the text that support your answer.

4. Use context to determine the meaning of the word **deprived** as it is used in the fable "The Hen and the Golden Eggs." Write your definition of *deprived* here and explain what you think it means, based on the word's context clues.

5. The Latin word *fervere* means "to boil." The Latin suffix *-ly,* which means "in what manner," is used in English for many adverbs. Use your knowledge of Latin roots and suffixes to determine the meaning of **fervently** in paragraph 5. Write your definition of *fervently* here, and explain how you figured out its meaning.

Copyright © BookheadEd Learning, LLC

# Skill:
# Theme

Use the Checklist to analyze Theme in "Aesop's Fables." Refer to the sample student annotations about Theme in the text.

## ••• CHECKLIST FOR THEME

In order to identify a theme or central idea in a text, note the following:

✓ the subject, topic, or genre of the text

✓ whether or not the theme is stated directly in the text

✓ details in the text that help to reveal theme

- a narrator's or speaker's tone
- title and chapter headings
- details about the setting
- characters' thoughts, actions, and dialogue
- the central conflict in the story's plot
- the resolution of the conflict

To determine a theme or central idea of a text and analyze its development over the course of the text, consider the following questions:

✓ What is a theme or central idea of the text?

✓ When did you become aware of that theme? For instance, did the story's conclusion reveal the theme?

✓ How does the theme develop over the course of the text?

# Skill:
# Theme

Reread "The Fox and the Woodcutter," paragraph 5 of "Aesop's Fables." Then, using the Checklist on the previous page, answer the multiple-choice questions below.

## ⟳ YOUR TURN

1. This question has two parts. First, answer Part A. Then, answer Part B.

   **Part A:** Which of the following statements **best** represents the fable's theme?

   ○ A. Good words are meaningless if you do not act honestly.

   ○ B. Keeping your body in shape is just as important as being smart.

   ○ C. Bad people can get away with crimes if they are smart.

   ○ D. Strangers can be just as helpful as friends when you are in danger.

   **Part B:** The detail that **best** reveals the theme identified in part A is—

   ○ A. the Woodcutter advises the Fox to take shelter in his own hut.

   ○ B. the huntsman takes no notice of the signs.

   ○ C. the Woodcutter says, "you owe your life to me."

   ○ D. the Fox says, "if your hands had not been traitors to your speech."

Please note that excerpts and passages in the StudySync® library and this workbook are intended as touchstones to generate interest in an author's work. The excerpts and passages do not substitute for the reading of entire texts, and StudySync® strongly recommends that students seek out and purchase the whole literary or informational work in order to experience it as the author intended. Links to online resellers are available in our digital library. In addition, complete works may be ordered through an authorized reseller by filling out and returning to StudySync® the order form enclosed in this workbook.

Reading & Writing Companion          **5**

# Close Read

Reread "Aesop's Fables." As you reread, complete the Skills Focus questions below. Then use your answers and annotations from the questions to help you complete the Write activity.

## ◎ SKILLS FOCUS

1. Reread "The Flies and the Honey-Pot" and "The Hen and the Golden Eggs." In each fable, identify the lesson and paraphrase it in your own words. Make sure to maintain the meaning and the logical order of the original text. Then explain how the lessons relate to an overall theme about life in general.

2. Identify a theme in one of the last four fables. Explain how this theme is similar to and different from a theme in another fable of your choice.

3. Recall that a miser is someone who hates to spend money. Identify evidence that the Miser has this quality, and explain how this quality influences the events of the fable.

4. The saying that someone is a "wolf in sheep's clothing" comes from the Aesop's fable of that name. Identify evidence of the Wolf's qualities, and explain how those qualities lead to the lesson of the fable.

5. Identify a lesson from one of the fables that is relevant to modern life. Explain an experience you've had that shows the relevance of this lesson.

## ✏ WRITE

NARRATIVE: Write a fable of your own that demonstrates a clear theme. Use a variety of writing techniques. Make sure to state a lesson at the end of your story as a moral that reflects your chosen theme. In your fable, include animal characters that have human traits.

The
Hunger
Games

FICTION
Suzanne Collins
2008

# Introduction

The *Hunger Games* is a dystopian novel by Suzanne Collins (b. 1962) set in fictional Panem, which is all that remains of post-apocalyptic North America in the not-too-distant future. In punishment for a failed uprising, the government annually requires each of the 12 districts of Panem to choose one boy and one girl to go to the Capitol, where they must participate in a televised battle to the death. At the selection ceremony for District 12, 16-year-old Katniss is horrified by a selection

# "The last tribute standing wins."

from Chapter 1

1   "You look beautiful," says Prim in a hushed voice.

2   "And nothing like myself," I say. I hug her, because I know these next few hours will be terrible for her. Her first reaping[1]. She's about as safe as you can get, since she's only entered once. I wouldn't let her take out any tesserae[2]. But she's worried about me. That the unthinkable might happen.

3   I protect Prim in every way I can, but I'm powerless against the reaping. The **anguish** I always feel when she's in pain wells up in my chest and threatens to register on my face. I notice her blouse has pulled out of her skirt in the back again and force myself to stay calm. "Tuck your tail in, little duck," I say, smoothing the blouse back in place.

4   Prim giggles and gives me a small "Quack."

5   "Quack yourself," I say with a light laugh. The kind only Prim can draw out of me. "Come on, let's eat," I say and plant a quick kiss on the top of her head.

· · ·

6   It's too bad, really, that they hold the reaping in the square—one of the few places in District 12 that can be pleasant. The square's surrounded by shops, and on public market days, especially if there's good weather, it has a holiday feel to it. But today, despite the bright banners hanging on the buildings, there's an air of grimness. The camera crews, perched like buzzards on rooftops, only add to the effect.

7   People file in silently and sign in. The reaping is a good opportunity for the Capitol to keep tabs on the population as well. Twelve- through eighteen-year-olds are herded into roped areas marked off by ages, the oldest in the

---

1. **reaping**  the gathering of candidates for the Hunger Games
2. **tesserae**  small wood, bone, or stone tablets used as vouchers or tokens that can be offered in exchange for being entered into a drawing to participate in the Hunger Games

front, the young ones, like Prim, toward the back. Family members line up around the perimeter, holding tightly to one another's hands. But there are others, too, who have no one they love at stake, or who no longer care, who slip among the crowd, taking bets on the two kids whose names will be drawn. Odds are given on their ages, whether they're Seam[3] or merchant, if they will break down and weep. Most refuse dealing with the racketeers but carefully, carefully. These same people tend to be informers, and who hasn't broken the law? I could be shot on a daily basis for hunting, but the appetites of those in charge protect me. Not everyone can claim the same.

. . .

8   Just as the town clock strikes two, the mayor steps up to the podium and begins to read. It's the same story every year. He tells of the history of Panem, the country that rose up out of the ashes of a place that was once called North America. He lists the disasters, the droughts, the storms, the fires, the **encroaching** seas that swallowed up so much of the land, the brutal war for what little sustenance remained. The result was Panem, a shining Capitol ringed by thirteen districts, which brought peace and prosperity to its citizens. Then came the Dark Days, the uprising of the districts against the Capitol. Twelve were defeated, the thirteenth obliterated. The Treaty of Treason gave us the new laws to **guarantee** peace and, as our yearly reminder that the Dark Days must never be repeated, it gave us the Hunger Games.

9   The rules of the Hunger Games are simple. In punishment for the uprising, each of the twelve districts must provide one girl and one boy, called tributes, to participate. The twenty-four tributes will be imprisoned in a vast outdoor arena that could hold anything from a burning desert to a frozen wasteland. Over a period of several weeks, the competitors must fight to the death. The last tribute standing wins.

10   Taking the kids from our districts, forcing them to kill one another while we watch—this is the Capitol's way of reminding us how totally we are at their mercy. How little chance we would stand of surviving another rebellion.

. . .

11   It's time for the drawing. Effie Trinket says as she always does, "Ladies first!" and crosses to the glass ball with the girls' names. She reaches in, digs her hand deep into the ball, and pulls out a slip of paper. The crowd draws in a collective breath and then you can hear a pin drop, and I'm feeling nauseous and so desperately hoping that it's not me, that it's not me, that it's not me.

---

3. **Seam** member of the poorest district in Panem

12   Effie Trinket crosses back to the podium, smoothes the slip of paper, and reads out the name in a clear voice. And it's not me.

13   It's Primrose Everdeen.

from Chapter 2

14   There must have been some mistake. This can't be happening. Prim was one slip of paper in thousands! Her chances of being chosen were so **remote** that I'd not even bothered worrying about her. Hadn't I done everything? Taken the tesserae, refused to let her do the same? One slip. One slip in thousands. The odds had been entirely in her favor. But it hadn't mattered.

15   Somewhere far away, I can hear the crowd murmuring unhappily as they always do when a twelve-year-old gets chosen because no one thinks this is fair. And then I see her, the blood drained from her face, hands clenched in fists at her sides, walking with stiff, small steps up toward the stage, passing me, and I see the back of her blouse has become untucked and hangs out over her skirt. It's this detail, the untucked blouse forming a ducktail, that brings me back to myself.

16   "Prim!" The strangled cry comes out of my throat, and my muscles begin to move again. "Prim!" I don't need to shove through the crowd. The other kids make way immediately allowing me a straight path to the stage. I reach her just as she is about to **mount** the steps. With one sweep of my arm, I push her behind me.

17   "I volunteer!" I gasp. "I volunteer as tribute!"

---

Excerpted from *The Hunger Games* by Suzanne Collins, published by Scholastic Inc.

 WRITE

PERSONAL RESPONSE: Were you surprised that Katniss offered to take her sister's place in the reaping? Write a short response explaining your initial reaction to the last scene of the excerpt. Use evidence from the text to support your response.

# The Classical Roots of 'The Hunger Games'

INFORMATIONAL TEXT
Barry Strauss
2014

## Introduction

Films in *The Hunger Games* series owe their success to more than just the series' leading actress, Jennifer Lawrence, or their exciting blend of action and dystopian political intrigue. As essayist Barry Strauss explains, the story also strikes a more "classical" chord of understanding about human nature. The heroine of *The Hunger Games*, Katniss Everdeen, is a combination of several Greek and Roman goddesses. In *The Hunger Games* author Suzanne Collins's own words, Katniss most closely recalls a female version of the Greek god Theseus, who slayed the Minotaur and saved young Athenians from being sacrificed to a horrific half-man, half-beast.

# "Like ancient gladiators, the participants are doomed but idolized."

NOTES

1   What accounts for the success of "The Hunger Games"? The obvious answer, of course, is the combination of the irresistible Jennifer Lawrence and Hollywood special effects with a **rollicking** good story.

2   But we shouldn't ignore the deeper themes of the tale, which are not only classic but classical, reaching back to Greece and Rome and the very foundations of Western culture.

3   At the heart of the story are three beautiful, heroic young people: Katniss Everdeen and her male romantic interests, Peeta Mellark and Gale Hawthorne. They form a love triangle, but they also represent, from the point of view of the ancients, an aroused citizenry banding together and fighting for freedom against an evil empire.

4   Katniss, played by Ms. Lawrence, is "an updated Theseus," according to the books' author, Suzanne Collins. In Greek myth, Theseus and other young people from Athens were sent as tribute—human sacrificial offerings—to King Minos in Crete. The king turned them over to the Minotaur, a murderous beast who was half-man and half-bull and lived in a maze or labyrinth. The intrepid Theseus killed the Minotaur and saved his countrymen.

5   Like that ancient Greek hero, Katniss defies an oppressive empire and sparks a revolution. But it's an update with a twist. Today's Theseus is female, which calls to mind not only modern girl power but also ancient lore. Her character is inspired by the famous Amazon warriors and Atalanta, the great female runner of Greek myth. Katniss also recalls Artemis, goddess of the hunt— Diana to the Romans—because her preferred weapon is the bow and arrow.

6   Like imperial Rome, the country of "The Hunger Games" is a once-free society now dominated by a **corrupt** and rapacious capital city. A president exercises, in effect, the power of an emperor. He lives in a grand city called the Capitol, and his government feeds off its provinces, much as ancient Rome did. The people of the Capitol radiate a baroque and overripe luxuriousness, like the lords and ladies of imperial Rome, while the provincials are poor and virtuous.

NOTES

7   This pattern goes back to the great Roman historian Tacitus (ca. 56–117), who drew a contrast between the primitive but free Germans and Britons and the decadent Romans who had lost their republican virtue under the Caesars. Tacitus would have understood why the bad guys in Ms. Collins's Capitol have Latinate first names such as Coriolanus Snow, the coldhearted president, and Caesar Flickerman, the smarmy host of the televised version of the games. Meanwhile, the rebels from the provinces have names that evoke nature ("katniss," for example, is the name of a real, edible plant) or have English or Greek roots—anything but Rome.

8   In "The Hunger Games," the people are kept in line by hunger and entertainment. The privileged folks in the Capitol get both "bread and circuses"—the phrase comes from the Roman satirist Juvenal[1]. The Latin is "panem et circenses," and Panem is the name that Ms. Collins purposefully gives the country where her story is set.

9   The most important entertainers are the participants in the hunger games, a fight to the death, reminiscent of the gladiatorial games of ancient Rome, whose influence Ms. Collins also cites. The games begin with the very Roman ritual of participants entering a stadium on chariots to the wild applause of the crowd. Like ancient gladiators, the participants are doomed but **idolized.**

10  Much as in the myth of Theseus, the participants in the hunger games are offered as tribute to the Capitol, one young man and one young woman from each district of the country. For the lone survivor, the games are a rite of passage. All ancient societies made young people go through such rites. In Athens, new warriors had to survive in the woods, and there is an echo of this in the hunger games, which are set in a jungle.

11  Myths work because their themes are of **abiding** interest, and "The Hunger Games" is no **exception.** We still have rites of passage for young people today. If ours tend to test mental rather than physical **stamina** (college entrance exams are more common than boot camps), they remain daunting and demanding in their own way—which perhaps explains why the life-or-death stakes of "The Hunger Games" strike such a deep chord among our decidedly nonclassical teens.

©2014 by Barry Strauss. Reproduced by permission of Barry Strauss.

1. **Juvenal** a Roman poet from the late first and early second century, C.E., who wrote a collection of satirical poems known as the *Satires*

**WRITE**

PERSONAL RESPONSE: According to the article, what are some of the story elements and themes that create a story that has "abiding interest"? Think about your favorite books, movies, and TV shows. Write a short response that describes how a modern-day book, movie, or TV show that you enjoy reflects at least one traditional story element or theme identified in the article.

# The Cruel Tribute

FICTION
James Baldwin
1895

## Introduction

James Baldwin (1841–1925) was a self-taught American who served as a superintendent at a school in Indianapolis, Indiana, before becoming a prolific author. He showed particular interest in history and legend, writing more than 30 books, many of which have been published in countries all around the globe. This particular legend is about the King of Crete and the revenge he seeks against the city of Athens, where his son was killed. In response to this incident the King of Crete demands, once every year, a "tribute" from Athens as repayment for the death of his son. Every spring, 14 youths are sent to Crete to be sacrificed—until a young

# "What is the tribute which you require?"

## I. THE TREATY.

1   Minos, king of Crete, had made war upon Athens. He had come with a great fleet of ships and an army, and had burned the merchant vessels in the harbor, and had overrun all the country and the coast even to Megara[1], which lies to the west. He had laid waste the fields and gardens round about Athens, had pitched his camp close to the walls, and had sent word to the Athenian rulers that on the morrow[2] he would march into their city with fire and sword and would slay all their young men and would pull down all their houses, even to the Temple of Athena, which stood on the great hill above the town. Then AEgeus, the king of Athens, with the twelve elders who were his helpers, went out to see King Minos and to treat with him.

2   "O mighty king," they said, "what have we done that you should wish thus to destroy us from the earth?"

3   "O cowardly and shameless men," answered King Minos, "why do you ask this foolish question, since you can but know the cause of my wrath? I had an only son, Androgeos by name, and he was dearer to me than the hundred cities of Crete and the thousand islands of the sea over which I rule. Three years ago he came hither to take part in the games which you held in honor of Athena, whose temple you have built on yonder hilltop. You know how he overcame all your young men in the sports, and how your people honored him with song and dance and laurel crown. But when your king, this same AEgeus who stands before me now, saw how everybody ran after him and praised his valor, he was filled with **envy** and laid plans to kill him. Whether he caused armed men to waylay[3] him on the road to Thebes, or whether as some say he sent him against a certain wild bull of your country to be slain by that beast, I know not; but you cannot **deny** that the young man's life was taken from him through the plotting of this AEgeus."

---

1. **Megara** a historic town in West Attica, Greece
2. **on the morrow** tomorrow
3. **waylay** to stop someone and hold them back for conversation or some other distraction

4    "But we do deny it—we do deny it!" cried the elders. "For at that very time our king was sojourning[4] at Troezen on the other side of the Saronic Sea, and he knew nothing of the young prince's death. We ourselves managed the city's affairs while he was abroad, and we know whereof we speak. Androgeos was slain, not through the king's orders but by the king's nephews, who hoped to rouse your anger against AEgeus so that you would drive him from Athens and leave the kingdom to one of them."

5    "Will you swear that what you tell me is true?" said Minos.

6    "We will swear it," they said.

7    "Now then," said Minos, "you shall hear my decree. Athens has robbed me of my dearest treasure, a treasure that can never be **restored** to me; so, in return, I **require** from Athens, as tribute, that possession which is the dearest and most precious to her people; and it shall be destroyed cruelly as my son was destroyed."

8    "The condition is hard," said the elders, "but it is just. What is the tribute which you require?"

9    "Has the king a son?" asked Minos.

10    The face of King AEgeus lost all its color and he trembled as he thought of a little child then with its mother at Troezen, on the other side of the Saronic Sea. But the elders knew nothing about that child, and they answered:

11    "Alas, no! he has no son; but he has fifty nephews who are eating up his substance and longing for the time to come when one of them shall be king; and, as we have said, it was they who slew the young prince, Androgeos."

12    "I have naught to do with those fellows," said Minos; "you may deal with them as you like. But you ask what is the tribute that I require, and I will tell you. Every year when the springtime comes and the roses begin to bloom, you shall choose seven of your noblest youths and seven of your fairest maidens, and shall send them to me in a ship which your king shall provide. This is the tribute which you shall pay to me, Minos, king of Crete; and if you fail for a single time, or delay even a day, my soldiers shall tear down your walls and burn your city and put your men to the sword and sell your wives and children as slaves."

13    "We agree to all this, O King," said the elders; "for it is the least of two evils. But tell us now, what shall be the fate of the seven youths and the seven maidens?"

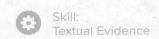

**Skill:**
Textual Evidence

*The text states that the elders knew nothing about the king's son. This implies that the king keeps secrets from the elders and acts selfishly. Note: the king's refusal to sacrifice his own son is what leads to the cruel tribute.*

---

4. **sojourning** temporarily visiting somewhere

14  "In Crete," answered Minos, "there is a house called the Labyrinth[5], the like of which you have never seen. In it there are a thousand chambers and winding ways, and whosoever goes even a little way into them can never find his way out again. Into this house the seven youths and the seven maidens shall be thrust, and they shall be left there—"

15  "To perish with hunger?" cried the elders.

16  "To be devoured by a monster whom men call the Minotaur," said Minos.

17  Then King AEgeus and the elders covered their faces and wept and went slowly back into the city to tell their people of the sad and terrible conditions upon which Athens could alone be saved.

18  "It is better that a few should perish than that the whole city should be destroyed," they said.

II. THE TRIBUTE.

19  Years passed by. Every spring when the roses began to bloom seven youths and seven maidens were put on board of a black-sailed ship and sent to Crete to pay the tribute which King Minos required. In every house in Athens there was sorrow and dread, and the people lifted up their hands to Athena on the hilltop and cried out, "How long, O Queen of the Air, how long shall this thing be?"

20  In the meanwhile the little child at Troezen on the other side of the sea had grown to be a man. His name, Theseus, was in everybody's mouth, for he had done great deeds of daring; and at last he had come to Athens to find his father, King AEgeus, who had never heard whether he was alive or dead; and when the youth had made himself known, the king had welcomed him to his home and all the people were glad because so noble a prince had come to dwell among them and, in time, to rule over their city.

21  The springtime came again. The black-sailed ship was rigged for another voyage. The rude Cretan soldiers paraded the streets; and the herald of King Minos stood at the gates and shouted:

22  "Yet three days, O Athenians, and your tribute will be due and must be paid!"

23  Then in every street the doors of the houses were shut and no man went in or out, but every one sat silent with pale cheeks, and wondered whose lot it

---

5. **Labyrinth** In Greek mythology, the Labyrinth was an elaborate building designed by the artist Daedalus for King Minos.

would be to be chosen this year. But the young prince, Theseus, did not understand; for he had not been told about the tribute.

24  "What is the meaning of all this?" he cried. "What right has a Cretan to demand tribute in Athens? and what is this tribute of which he speaks?"

25  Then AEgeus led him aside and with tears told him of the sad war with King Minos, and of the dreadful terms of peace. "Now, say no more," sobbed AEgeus, "it is better that a few should die even thus than that all should be destroyed."

26  "But I will say more," cried Theseus. "Athens shall not pay tribute to Crete. I myself will go with these youths and maidens, and I will slay the monster Minotaur, and defy King Minos himself upon his throne."

27  "Oh, do not be so rash!" said the king; "for no one who is thrust into the den of the Minotaur ever comes out again. Remember that you are the hope of Athens, and do not take this great risk upon yourself."

28  "Say you that I am the hope of Athens?" said Theseus. "Then how can I do otherwise than go?" And he began at once to make himself ready.

29  On the third day all the youths and maidens of the city were brought together in the market place, so that lots[6] might be cast for those who were to be taken. Then two vessels of brass were brought and set before King AEgeus and the herald who had come from Crete. Into one vessel they placed as many balls as there were noble youths in the city, and into the other as many as there were maidens; and all the balls were white save only seven in each vessel, and those were black as ebony.

30  Then every maiden, without looking, reached her hand into one of the vessels and drew forth a ball, and those who took the black balls were borne away to the black ship, which lay in waiting by the shore. The young men also drew lots in like manner, but when six black balls had been drawn Theseus came quickly forward and said:

31  "Hold! Let no more balls be drawn. I will be the seventh youth to pay this tribute. Now let us go aboard the black ship and be off."

32  Then the people, and King AEgeus himself, went down to the shore to take leave of the young men and maidens, whom they had no hope of seeing again; and all but Theseus wept and were brokenhearted.

**Skill:**
Textual Evidence

*Theseus's words imply that he is patriotic and daring. The king's answer implies that he is still being selfish, trying to save his own son. Theseus says he has no choice but to go. The implied meaning is that he is a noble, unselfish hero.*

---

6. **lots** objects randomly drawn from a container as part of a decision-making process.

NOTES

33 "I will come again, father," he said.

34 "I will hope that you may," said the old king. "If when this ship returns, I see a white sail spread above the black one, then I shall know that you are alive and well; but if I see only the black one, it will tell me that you have perished."

35 And now the vessel was loosed from its moorings, the north wind filled the sail, and the seven youths and seven maidens were borne away over the sea, towards the dreadful death which awaited them in far distant Crete.

III. THE PRINCESS.

36 At last the black ship reached the end of its voyage. The young people were set ashore, and a party of soldiers led them through the streets towards the prison, where they were to stay until the morrow. They did not weep nor cry out now, for they had outgrown their fears. But with paler faces and firm-set lips, they walked between the rows of Cretan houses, and looked neither to the right nor to the left. The windows and doors were full of people who were eager to see them.

37 "What a pity that such brave young men should be food for the Minotaur," said some.

38 "Ah, that maidens so beautiful should meet a fate so sad!" said others.

39 And now they passed close by the palace gate, and in it stood King Minos himself, and his daughter Ariadne, the fairest of the women of Crete.

40 "Indeed, those are noble young fellows!" said the king.

41 "Yes, too noble to feed the vile Minotaur," said Ariadne.

42 "The nobler, the better," said the king; "and yet none of them can compare with your lost brother Androgeos."

43 Ariadne said no more; and yet she thought that she had never seen any one who looked so much like a hero as young Theseus. How tall he was, and how handsome! How proud his eye, and how firm his step! Surely there had never been his like in Crete.

44 All through that night Ariadne lay awake and thought of the matchless hero, and grieved that he should be doomed to perish; and then she began to lay plans for setting him free. At the earliest peep of day she arose, and while everybody else was asleep, she ran out of the palace and hurried to the prison. As she was the king's daughter, the jailer opened the door at her bidding and allowed her to go in. There sat the seven youths and the seven

maidens on the ground, but they had not lost hope. She took Theseus aside and whispered to him. She told him of a plan which she had made to save him; and Theseus promised her that, when he had slain the Minotaur, he would carry her away with him to Athens where she should live with him always. Then she gave him a sharp sword, and hid it underneath his cloak, telling him that with it alone could he hope to slay the Minotaur.

45 "And here is a ball of silken thread," she said. "As soon as you go into the Labyrinth where the monster is kept, fasten one end of the thread to the stone doorpost, and then unwind it as you go along. When you have slain the Minotaur, you have only to follow the thread and it will lead you back to the door. In the meanwhile I will see that your ship, is ready to sail, and then I will wait for you at the door of the Labyrinth."

46 Theseus thanked the beautiful princess and promised her again that if he should live to go back to Athens she should go with him and be his wife. Then with a prayer to Athena, Ariadne hastened away.

IV. THE LABYRINTH.

47 As soon as the sun was up the guards came to lead the young prisoners to the Labyrinth. They did not see the sword which Theseus had under his cloak, nor the tiny ball of silk which he held in his closed hand. They led the youths and maidens a long way into the Labyrinth, turning here and there, back and forth, a thousand different times, until it seemed certain that they could never find their way out again. Then the guards, by a secret passage which they alone knew, went out and left them, as they had left many others before, to wander about until they should be found by the terrible Minotaur.

48 "Stay close by me," said Theseus to his companions, "and with the help of Athena who dwells in her temple home in our own fair city, I will save you."

49 Then he drew his sword and stood in the narrow way before them; and they all lifted up their hands and prayed to Athena.

50 For hours they stood there, hearing no sound, and seeing nothing but the smooth, high walls on either side of the passage and the calm blue sky so high above them. Then the maidens sat down upon the ground and covered their faces and sobbed, and said:

51 "Oh, that he would come and put an end to our misery and our lives."

52 At last, late in the day, they heard a **bellowing**, low and faint as though far away. They listened and soon heard it again, a little louder and very fierce and dreadful.

NOTES

53    "It is he! it is he!" cried Theseus; "and now for the fight!"

54    Then he shouted, so loudly that the walls of the Labyrinth answered back, and the sound was carried upward to the sky and outward to the rocks and cliffs of the mountains. The Minotaur heard him, and his bellowings grew louder and fiercer every moment.

55    "He is coming!" cried Theseus, and he ran forward to meet the beast. The seven maidens shrieked, but tried to stand up bravely and face their fate; and the six young men stood together with firm-set teeth and clinched fists, ready to fight to the last.

56    Soon the Minotaur came into view, rushing down the passage towards Theseus, and roaring most terribly. He was twice as tall as a man, and his head was like that of a bull with huge sharp horns and fiery eyes and a mouth as large as a lion's; but the young men could not see the lower part of his body for the cloud of dust which he raised in running. When he saw Theseus with the sword in his hand coming to meet him, he paused, for no one had ever faced him in that way before. Then he put his head down, and rushed forward, bellowing. But Theseus leaped quickly aside, and made a sharp thrust with his sword as he passed, and hewed off one of the monster's legs above the knee.

Theseus killed the Minotaur, a half-man, half-bull monster that lived in the Labyrinth.

57    The Minotaur fell upon the ground, roaring and groaning and beating wildly about with his horned head and his hoof-like fists; but Theseus **nimbly** ran up to him and thrust the sword into his heart, and was away again before the beast could harm him. A great stream of blood gushed from the wound, and soon the Minotaur turned his face towards the sky and was dead.

58    Then the youths and maidens ran to Theseus and kissed his hands and feet, and thanked him for his great deed; and, as it was already growing dark, Theseus bade[7] them follow him while he wound up the silken thread which was to lead them out of the Labyrinth. Through a thousand rooms and courts and winding ways they went, and at midnight they came to the outer door and saw the city lying in the moonlight before them; and, only a little way off, was the seashore where the black ship was moored which had brought them to Crete. The door was wide open, and beside it stood Ariadne waiting for them.

---

7. **bade** invited

59 "The wind is fair, the sea is smooth, and the sailors are ready," she whispered; and she took the arm of Theseus, and all went together through the silent streets to the ship.

60 When the morning dawned they were far out to sea, and, looking back from the deck of the little vessel, only the white tops of the Cretan mountains were in sight.

61 Minos, when he arose from sleep, did not know that the youths and maidens had gotten safe out of the Labyrinth. But when Ariadne could not be found, he thought that robbers had carried her away. He sent soldiers out to search for her among the hills and mountains, never dreaming that she was now well on the way towards distant Athens.

62 Many days passed, and at last the searchers returned and said that the princess could nowhere be found. Then the king covered his head and wept, and said:

63 "Now, indeed, I am bereft of all my treasures!"

64 In the meanwhile, King AEgeus of Athens had sat day after day on a rock by the shore, looking and watching if by chance he might see a ship coming from the south. At last the vessel with Theseus and his companions hove in sight, but it still carried only the black sail, for in their joy the young men had forgotten to raise the white one.

65 "Alas! alas! my son has perished!" moaned AEgeus; and he fainted and fell forward into the sea and was drowned. And that sea, from then until now, has been called by his name, the Aegean Sea.

66 Thus Theseus became king of Athens.

# First Read

Read "The Cruel Tribute." After you read, complete the Think Questions below.

Copyright © BookheadEd Learning, LLC

## ☁ THINK QUESTIONS

1. Why did AEgeus's nephews kill Androgeos, son of Minos? Briefly describe what they hoped to achieve. Did their plan work as expected? Be sure to cite textual evidence to support your response.

2. Why does Minos demand that fourteen Athenian youths be sent every year as tribute? What kind of tribute would he rather have, but cannot get? Cite textual evidence to support your response.

3. Why does Ariadne decide to help Theseus and the rest of the Athenian tributes? Does she have a specific motive for rescuing this group of tributes, or has she always been against the demands of her father? Be sure to cite textual evidence in your response.

4. Use context clues to determine the meaning of **bellowing** as it is used in paragraph 52 of "The Cruel Tribute." Write your definition here and identify clues that helped you figure out the meaning. Then check the meaning in a dictionary.

5. Find the word **nimbly** in paragraph 57 of "The Cruel Tribute." Use context clues in the surrounding sentences, as well as the sentence in which the word appears, to determine the word's meaning. Write your definition here and identify clues that helped you figure out the meaning.

# Skill:
# Textual Evidence

Use the Checklist to analyze Textual Evidence in "The Cruel Tribute." Refer to the sample student annotations about Textual Evidence in the text.

## ••• CHECKLIST FOR TEXTUAL EVIDENCE

In order to support an analysis by citing textual evidence that is explicitly stated in the text, do the following:

✓ read the text closely and critically

✓ identify what the text says explicitly

✓ find the most relevant textual evidence that supports your analysis

✓ consider why an author explicitly states specific details and information

✓ cite the specific words, phrases, sentences, paragraphs, or images from the text that support your analysis

In order to interpret implicit meanings in a text by making inferences, do the following:

✓ combine information directly stated in the text with your own knowledge, experiences, and observations

✓ cite the specific words, phrases, sentences, paragraphs, or images from the text that support this inference

In order to cite textual evidence to support an analysis of what the text says explicitly as well as inferences drawn from the text, consider the following questions:

✓ Have I read the text closely and critically?

✓ What inferences am I making about the text? What textual evidence am I using to support these inferences?

✓ Am I quoting the evidence from the text correctly?

✓ Does my textual evidence logically relate to my analysis?

✓ Have I cited several pieces of textual evidence?

# Skill:
# Textual Evidence

Reread paragraphs 61–66 of "The Cruel Tribute." Then, using the Checklist on the previous page, answer the multiple-choice questions below.

## ↻ YOUR TURN

1. Paragraphs 61 to 63 tell what King Minos does when Ariadne cannot be found. Readers can infer from these actions that —

   ○ A. the king is not aware that his daughter helped Theseus and his companions escape.
   ○ B. the king is kept informed of everything that goes on inside the Labyrinth.
   ○ C. the king cares more about his daughter than he once cared about his son.
   ○ D. King Minos realizes that he is being punished for demanding the cruel tribute.

2. Paragraphs 64 and 65 tell what happens to King AEgeus when Theseus comes home. Readers can infer from these events that —

   ○ A. AEgeus knows that he is being punished for his original refusal to sacrifice his own son.
   ○ B. AEgeus recognizes his son as a hero and has faith that he has overcome the Minotaur.
   ○ C. AEgeus dies because he placed so much value on his son.
   ○ D. Theseus would probably have remembered to raise the white sail before reaching the shore.

3. The resolution (the way that the story ends) implies that in the future Athens will —

   ○ A. no longer be threatened by King Minos of Crete.
   ○ B. have royal princes who will become rulers of Crete.
   ○ C. give greater power to the elders and less power to kings.
   ○ D. be ruled by a more courageous and selfless king.

# Close Read

Reread "The Cruel Tribute." As you reread, complete the Skills Focus questions below. Then use your answers and annotations from the questions to help you complete the Write activity.

## ◎ SKILLS FOCUS

1. Select a character. Identify a detail that shows that character's key qualities. Explain how that character's qualities influence the events of the story.

2. Identify important setting details in the Labyrinth. Explain how the setting of the Labyrinth affects the characters and plot.

3. "The Classical Roots of 'The Hunger Games'" uses Katniss of *The Hunger Games* as an example of a classically heroic figure. Identify heroic traits in Theseus, and explain how his traits reflect themes of what makes a hero.

4. Identify elements of "The Cruel Tribute" that you can recall appearing in *The Hunger Games* or being singled out in "The Classical Roots of 'The Hunger Games.'" Give your opinion as to why these specific elements are of such lasting importance.

## ✎ WRITE

COMPARE AND CONTRAST: Compare and contrast a character from "The Cruel Tribute" with a character from the excerpt of *The Hunger Games* based on what the texts say implicitly and explicitly about the characters. Remember to use evidence from each text to support your claims.

# The Invisible One

(Algonquin Cinderella)

**FICTION**
Traditional Algonquin
(collected by Idries Shah)
1979

## Introduction

In his expansive collection of folklore, *World Tales*, author and educator Idries Shah (1924–1996) gives credit, in particular, to the work of Marian Roalfe Cox. Late in the 19th century, Cox spent a year gathering more than 300 Cinderella-like tales from traditions and cultures around the world. One of those is the tale presented here, "The Invisible One," which comes from the MicMac Indians of the Eastern Algonquins. It is the story of an invisible man residing in a village who can be seen only by his sister and one other girl, the one who will have the opportunity to marry him. One after another, the girls of the village take a test to try to see the Invisible One. Each of them fails until an unassuming young girl, cast aside by her haughty older sisters

# "She would try, she thought, to . . . see the Invisible One."

1   There was once a large village of the MicMac Indians of the Eastern Algonquins, built beside a lake. At the far end of the **settlement** stood a lodge, and in it lived a being who was always invisible. He had a sister who looked after him, and everyone knew that any girl who could see him might marry him. For that reason there were very few girls who did not try, but it was very long before anyone succeeded.

2   This is the way in which the test of sight was carried out: at evening time, when the Invisible One was due to be returning home, his sister would walk with any girl who might come down to the lakeshore. She, of course, could see her brother, since he was always **visible** to her. As soon as she saw him, she would say to the girls:

3   "Do you see my brother?"

4   "Yes," they would generally reply—though some of them did say, "No."

5   To those who said that they could indeed see him, the sister would say:

6   "Of what is his shoulder strap made?" Some people say that she would enquire:

7   "What is his moose-runner's haul?" or "With what does he draw his sled?"

8   And they would answer:

9   "A strip of rawhide[1]," or "a green **flexible** branch," or something like that.

10  Then she, knowing that they had not told the truth, would say:

11  "Very well, let us return to the wigwam![2]"

12  When they had gone in, she would tell them not to sit in a certain place, because it belonged to the Invisible One. Then, after they had helped to

---

1. **rawhide**  stiff, untanned leather
2. **wigwam**  a dome-shaped structure made by fastening material over a framework of poles, used by some North American indigenous peoples

NOTES

Skill:
Summarizing

*Who? the Invisible One, his sister, and the other villagers*

*What? The sister tests the other girls.*

*Where? the village*

*When? in the evening*

*Why? to help the Invisible One find a wife*

*How? The girl who can see the Invisible One might marry him.*

**Skill:**
Plot

*I can tell that the sisters are going to be important characters in the story. They treat Oochigeaskw really badly. The conflict between the sisters will be important in the plot.*

cook the supper, they would wait with great **curiosity,** to see him eat. They could be sure that he was a real person, for when he took off his moccasins[3] they became visible, and his sister hung them up. But beyond this, they saw nothing of him, not even when they stayed in the place all night, as many of them did.

13 Now there lived in the village an old man who was a widower, and his three daughters. The youngest girl was very small, weak and often ill: and yet her sisters, especially the elder, treated her cruelly. The second daughter was kinder, and sometimes took her side: but the wicked sister would burn her hands and feet with hot cinders, and she was covered with scars from this treatment. She was so marked that people called her *Oochigeaskw*, the Rough-Faced Girl.

14 When her father came home and asked why she had such burns, the bad sister would at once say that it was her own fault, for she had disobeyed orders and gone near the fire and fallen into it.

15 These two elder sisters decided one day to try their luck at seeing the Invisible One. So they dressed themselves in their finest clothes, and tried to look their prettiest. They found the Invisible One's sister and took the usual walk by the water.

16 When he came, and when they were asked if they could see him, they answered, "Of course." And when asked about the shoulder strap or sled cord, they answered: "A piece of rawhide."

17 But of course they were lying like the others, and they got nothing for their pains.

18 The next afternoon, when the father returned home, he brought with him many of the pretty little shells from which wampum[4] was made, and they set to work to string them.

19 That day, poor little Oochigeaskw, who had always gone barefoot, got a pair of her father's moccasins, old ones, and put them into water to soften them so that she could wear them. Then she begged her sisters for a few wampum shells. The elder called her a 'little pest', but the younger one gave her some. Now, with no other clothes than her usual rags, the poor little thing went into the woods and got herself some sheets of birch bark, from which she made a dress, and put marks on it for decoration, in the style of long ago. She made a petticoat and a loose gown, a cap, leggings and a handkerchief. She put on her father's large old moccasins, which were far too big for her, and went

---

3. **moccasin**  a soft leather shoe, having the sole turned up on all sides and sewn to the top in a simple gathered seam
4. **wampum**  small beads strung together and worn as jewelry or used as money

forth to try her luck. She would try, she thought, to discover whether she could see the Invisible One.

20  She did not begin very well. As she set off, her sisters shouted and hooted, hissed and yelled, and tried to make her stay. And the loafers around the village, seeing the strange little creature, called out "Shame!"

21  The poor little girl in her strange clothes, with her face all scarred, was an awful sight, but she was kindly received by the sister of the Invisible One. And this was, of course, because this noble lady understood far more about things than simply the **mere** outside which all the rest of the world knows. As the brown of the evening sky turned to black, the lady took her down to the lake.

22  "Do you see him?" the Invisible One's sister asked.

23  "I do, indeed—and he is wonderful!" said Oochigeaskw.

24  The sister asked:

25  "And what is his sled string?"

26  The little girl said:

27  "It is the Rainbow."

28  "And, my sister, what is his bow string?"

29  "It is The Spirit's Road—the Milky Way."

30  "So you *have* seen him," said his sister. She took the girl home with her and bathed her. As she did so, all the scars disappeared from her body. Her hair grew again, as it was combed, long, like a blackbird's wing. Her eyes were now like stars: in all the world there was no other such beauty. Then, from her treasures, the lady gave her a wedding garment, and adorned her.

31  Then she told Oochigeaskw to take the *wife's* seat in the wigwam, the one next to where the Invisible One sat, beside the entrance. And when he came in, terrible and beautiful, he smiled and said:

32  "So we are found out!"

33  "Yes," said his sister. And so Oochigeaskw became his wife.

Skill: Plot

*The older sisters are so mean and don't want their sister to try to discover if she can see the Invisible One. Some of the villagers are being awful too! This seems like it could be the turning point in the story.*

# First Read

Read "The Invisible One." After you read, complete the Think Questions below.

1. How is Oochigeaskw treated by her older sisters? Explain, citing specific details from the text.

2. How does the Invisible One's sister administer the test of sight? What happens to most of the girls who take the test before Oochigeaskw? Explain.

3. What happens to Oochigeaskw after she recognizes the Invisible One? Describe how her life changes after this fateful moment.

4. Which context clues helped you determine the meaning of the word **flexible** as it is used in paragraph 9? Write your own definition of *flexible* and identify which words or phrases helped you understand its meaning.

5. The Greek word *meros* refers to a "part" or "fraction." Using this information, what do you think is the meaning of the word **mere** in paragraph 21? Write your best definition of *mere* and explain how you figured it out.

# Skill:
# Summarizing

Use the Checklist to analyze Summarizing in "The Invisible One." Refer to the sample student annotations about Summarizing in the text.

## ••• CHECKLIST FOR SUMMARIZING

In order to determine how to write an objective summary of a text, note the following:

- ✓ in literature, note the setting, characters, and events in the plot, including the problem the characters face and how it is solved

- ✓ answers to the basic questions *who, what, where, when, why,* and *how*

- ✓ stay objective, and do not add your own personal thoughts, judgments, or opinions to the summary

To provide an objective summary of a text, consider the following questions:

- ✓ What are the answers to basic *who, what, where, when, why,* and *how* questions in literature and works of nonfiction?

- ✓ In a work of literature, do the details in my summary reflect the development of the theme?

- ✓ Is my summary objective, or have I added my own thoughts, judgments, and personal opinions?

# Skill:
# Summarizing

Reread paragraphs 13–19 of "The Invisible One" and the important details below. Then, complete the chart by sorting the important details into the correct category to objectively summarize what happened in the excerpt.

## ⟳ YOUR TURN

| | Important Details |
|---|---|
| **A** | So that they could marry the Invisible One |
| **B** | In the village by the lake |
| **C** | A father and his three daughters, the youngest of whom was very weak and treated unkindly |
| **D** | One evening and the next day |
| **E** | By dressing up in their finest clothes and walking by the water |
| **F** | The sisters decided to discover if they could see the Invisible One. |

| Who | What | Where | When | Why | How |
|---|---|---|---|---|---|
| | | | | | |

# PLOT

## Skill: Plot

Use the Checklist to analyze Plot in "The Invisible One." Refer to the sample student annotations about Plot in the text.

## ••• CHECKLIST FOR PLOT

In order to identify particular elements of a story or drama, note the following:

- ✓ setting details

- ✓ character details, including their thoughts, actions, and descriptions

- ✓ notable incidents or events in the plot

- ✓ characters or setting details that may have caused an event to occur

- ✓ the central conflict and the characters who are involved

- ✓ dialogue between or among characters

- ✓ instances when setting interferes with a character's motivations

To analyze how particular elements of a story or drama interact, consider the following questions:

- ✓ How do the events of the plot unfold in the story?

- ✓ How do characters respond or change as the plot advances?

- ✓ How does the setting shape the characters or the plot?

- ✓ How does a particular scene in the story contribute to the development of the plot?

# PLOT

## Skill: Plot

Reread paragraphs 21–33 of "The Invisible One." Then, using the Checklist on the previous page, answer the multiple-choice questions below.

## ↻ YOUR TURN

1. This question has two parts. First, answer Part A. Then, answer Part B.

    **Part A:** Which character action or dialogue leads to the story's resolution?

    ○ A. The moment when the Invisible One's sister takes Oochigeaskw to the lake in the evening

    ○ B. The moment when Oochigeaskw bathes and her hair grows, all her scars disappear, and she is given a wedding garment

    ○ C. The moment when the Invisible One's sister tells Oochigeaskw to take the wife's seat

    ○ D. The moment when Oochigeaskw correctly identifies the Invisible One's sled and bowstring to the sister

    **Part B:** Which of the following details BEST supports your response to Part A?

    ○ A. The Invisible One's sister asks about the sled bow string to test Oochigeaskw.

    ○ B. When he came into the wigwam, he smiled at her and she became his wife.

    ○ C. After Oochigeaskw answers, the sister says, "So you *have* seen him."

    ○ D. Her scars magically healed, her hair regrew, and her eyes became like stars.

# Close Read

Reread "The Invisible One." As you reread, complete the Skills Focus questions below. Then use your answers and annotations from the questions to help you complete the Write activity.

## ◎ SKILLS FOCUS

1. Identify examples of how the behavior of the Invisible One's sister further develops her character at the beginning of the story.

2. Objectively summarize the beginning, the middle, and the end of the story. Include the most important details.

3. Most of the village girls try their luck at seeing the Invisible One. Identify an event in the text and explain how it encourages Oochigeaskw to try to see the Invisible One.

4. A common theme in folktales is that goodness is rewarded. Identify a moment in "The Invisible One" in which goodness is rewarded, and explain how this theme makes myths and folktales appealing to readers today.

## ✏ WRITE

NARRATIVE: Write your own version of a Cinderella story using a variety of techniques such as descriptive details and dialogue. Plan out the story to include clear plot events including an inciting incident, a conflict, and a turning point, leading to the resolution of the story.

Please note that excerpts and passages in the StudySync® library and this workbook are intended as touchstones to generate interest in an author's work. The excerpts and passages do not substitute for the reading of entire texts, and StudySync® strongly recommends that students seek out and purchase the whole literary or informational work in order to experience it as the author intended. Links to online resellers are available in our digital library. In addition, complete works may be ordered through an authorized reseller by filling out and returning to StudySync® the order form enclosed in this workbook.

Reading & Writing Companion    37

# The Other Side of the Sky

INFORMATIONAL TEXT
Farah Ahmedi and Tamim Ansary
2006

## Introduction

studysync

Farah Ahmedi's memoir *The Other Side of the Sky* is a testament to the power of the human spirit. Missing a leg after stepping on a landmine when she was seven, and with her father and brothers dead from a rocket attack, Ahmedi and her mother decide to flee their home in Kabul in search of a better life. This excerpt from "Escape from Afghanistan" describes their efforts to make it across the border and into Pakistan.

# "Night was falling, and we were stranded out there in the open."

from: Escape from Afghanistan

NOTES

⚙ Skill:
Textual Evidence

*The narrator uses the word desperate when she describes trying to get through the gate. This tells me exactly how the narrator and the people around her must have felt in that moment. They were desperate for freedom.*

1   The gate to Pakistan was closed, and I could see that the Pakistani border guards were letting no one through. People were pushing and shoving and jostling up against that gate, and the guards were driving them back. As we got closer, the crowd thickened, and I could hear the roar and clamor at the gate. The Afghans were yelling something, and the Pakistanis were yelling back. My mother was clutching her side and gasping for breath, trying to keep up. I felt desperate to get through, because the sun was setting, and if we got stuck here, what were we going to do? Where would we stay? There was nothing here, no town, no hotel, no buildings, just the desert.

2   Yet we had no real chance of getting through. Big strong men were running up to the gate in vain. The guards had clubs, and they had carbines, too, which they turned around and used as weapons. Again and again, the crowd surged toward the gate and the guards drove them back with their sticks and clubs, swinging and beating until the crowd **receded**. And after that, for the next few minutes, on our side of the border, people milled about and muttered and stoked their own impatience and worked up their rage, until gradually the crowd gathered strength and surged against that gate again, only to be swept back.

3   We never even got close to the front. We got caught up in the thinning rear end of crowd, and even so, we were part of each wave, pulled forward, driven back. It was hard for me to keep my footing, and my mother was clutching my arm now, just hanging on, just trying to stay close to me, because the worst thing would have been if we had gotten separated. Finally, I saw that it was no use. We were only risking injury. We drifted back, out of the crowd. In the thickening dusk we could hear the dull roar of people still trying to get past the border guards, but we receded into the desert, farther and farther back from the border gate.

4   Night was falling, and we were stranded out there in the open.

. . .

**Skill:**
**Textual Evidence**

*The guards are taking bribes to let the people through. People are so desperate to leave that they will pay to get out. But the narrator and her mother do not have money to pay, so they must feel even worse. Freedom comes at a high price!*

5   On that second day, however, I learned that it was all a question of money. Someone told me about this, and then I watched closely and saw that it was true. Throughout the day, while some of the guards confronted the crowds, a few others lounged over to the side. People approached them quietly. Money changed hands, and the guards then let those people quietly through a small door to the side.

6   Hundreds could have flowed through the main gate had it been opened, but only one or two could get through the side door at a time. The fact that the guards were taking bribes[1] did us no good whatsoever. We did not have the money to pay them. What little we had we would need to get from Peshawar to Quetta. And so the second day passed.

7   At the end of that day we found ourselves camping near a friendly family. We struck up a conversation with them. The woman told us that her husband, Ghulam Ali, had gone to look for another way across the border. He was checking out a goat path that supposedly went over the mountains several miles northeast of the border station. If one could get to Pakistan safely by that route, he would come back for his family. "You can go with us," the woman said.

8   Later that night her husband showed up. "It works," he said. "Smugglers[2] use that path, and they bribe the guards to leave it unguarded. Of course, we don't want to run into any smugglers, either, but if we go late at night, we should be fine."

9   His wife then told him our story, and Ghulam Ali took pity on us. "Yes, of course you can come with us," he said. "But you have had two hard days. You will need some rest before you attempt this mountain crossing. Spend tonight here and sleep well, knowing that you will have nothing to do tomorrow except lounge around, rest, and catch your breath. Tomorrow, do not throw yourself against those border guards again. Let your only work be the gathering of your strength. Then tomorrow night we will all go over the mountain together, with God's grace. I will show you the way. If God wills it, we will follow that smugglers' path to safety. You and your mother are in my care now."

10   So we spent the whole next day there. It was terribly warm and we had no water, but we walked a little way and found a mosque[3] that refugees[4] like us had built over the years, so that people waiting to get across the border would have a place to say their prayers. We got some water to drink at the mosque, and we said *namaz*[5] there too. Somehow we obtained a little bit of bread as well. I can't remember how that turned up, but there it was, and we

---

1. **bribe**  an offer of money or another incentive to persuade someone to do something
2. **smugglers**  people who transfer items illegally into or out of an area
3. **mosque**  a Muslim house of worship
4. **refugees**  people forced to flee their own country to escape danger or persecution
5. *namaz*  Islamic worship or prayer

ate it. We **sustained** our strength. After sunset we lay down just as if we're going to spend another night. In fact, I did fall asleep for a while. Long after dark—or early the next morning, to be exact, before the sun came up—that man shook us awake. "It's time," he said.

11 We got up and performed our **ablutions** quickly in the darkness, with just sand because that's allowed when you have no access to water. We said our prayers. Then Ghulam Ali began to march into the darkness with his family, and we trudged along silently behind them. After several miles the path began to climb, and my mother began to wheeze. Her asthma was pretty bad at this point, poor thing. No doubt, her anxiety made it worse, but in such circumstances how could she rid herself of anxiety? It was no use knowing that her difficulty was rooted in anxiety, just as it was no use knowing that we could have moved more quickly if we had possessed wings. Life is what it is. The path over that mountain was not actually very long, only a couple of miles. Steep as it was, we could have gotten over in little more than an hour if not for my mother. Because of her, we had to pause every few minutes, so our journey took many hours.

12 I myself hardly felt the exertion. I was walking quite well that day, quite athletically. I had that good **prosthetic** leg from Germany. The foot was a little worn by then, but not enough to slow me down. Thinking back, I'm puzzled, actually. How did I scale that mountain so easily? How did I climb down the other side? These days I find it hard to clamber up two or three flights of stairs, even. I don't know what made me so **supple** and strong that day, but I felt no hardship, no anxiety or fear, just concentration and intensity. Perhaps my mother's problems distracted me from my own. That might account for it. Perhaps desperation gave me energy and made me forget the **rigor** of the climb. Well, whatever the reason, I scrambled up like a goat. The family we were following had a girl only a bit younger than me, and she was moving slowly. Her family used my example to chide her. They kept saying, "Look at that girl. She's missing a leg, and yet she's going faster than you. Why can't you keep up? Hurry now!"

13 That Ghulam Ali was certainly a good man, so patient with us and so compassionate. He had never seen us before, and yet when he met us, he said, "I will help you." That's the thing about life. You never know when and where you will encounter a spot of human decency. I have felt alone in this world at times; I have known long periods of being no one. But then, without warning, a person like Ghulam Ali just turns up and says, "I see you. I am on your side." Strangers have been kind to me when it mattered most. That sustains a person's hope and faith.

---

Excerpted from *The Other Side of the Sky* by Farah Ahmedi, published by Simon & Schuster.

# First Read

Read *The Other Side of the Sky*. After you read, complete the Think Questions below.

1.  Why were Ahmedi and her mother near the gate to the Pakistani border? Why couldn't they get any nearer to the gate? Cite specific evidence from the text to support your answer.

2.  What did Ahmedi learn on the second day about why a few people were being allowed to enter Pakistan? Why didn't this knowledge help her and her mother? Cite specific evidence from the text to support your response.

3.  What physical challenges did Ahmedi and her mother face as they crossed the mountain? Why was Ahmedi puzzled by her own physical abilities during the mountain crossing? Cite specific evidence from the text to support your response.

4.  Use context clues to determine the meaning of **supple** as it is used in the text. Then write your definition of *supple* here and check a print or online dictionary to confirm your definition.

5.  The Latin word *recedere* means "to go back." With this information in mind, write your best definition of **receded** here and explain how you figured out its meaning.

# Skill:
# Textual Evidence

Use the Checklist to analyze Textual Evidence in *The Other Side of the Sky*. Refer to the sample student annotations about Textual Evidence in the text.

## ••• CHECKLIST FOR TEXTUAL EVIDENCE

In order to support an analysis by citing textual evidence that is explicitly stated in the text, do the following:

- ✓ read the text closely and critically

- ✓ identify what the text says explicitly

- ✓ find the most relevant textual evidence that supports your analysis

- ✓ consider why an author explicitly states specific details and information

- ✓ cite the specific words, phrases, sentences, paragraphs, or images from the text that support your analysis

In order to interpret implicit meanings in a text by making inferences, do the following:

- ✓ combine information directly stated in the text with your own knowledge, experiences, and observations

- ✓ cite the specific words, phrases, sentences, paragraphs, or images from the text that support this inference

In order to cite textual evidence to support an analysis of what the text says explicitly as well as inferences drawn from the text, consider the following questions:

- ✓ Have I read the text closely and critically?

- ✓ What inferences am I making about the text? What textual evidence am I using to support these inferences?

- ✓ Am I quoting the evidence from the text correctly?

- ✓ Does my textual evidence logically relate to my analysis?

- ✓ Have I cited several pieces of textual evidence?

# Skill:
# Textual Evidence

Reread paragraphs 10–11 of *The Other Side of the Sky*. Then, using the Checklist on the previous page, answer the multiple-choice questions below.

## ⟳ YOUR TURN

1. Text details in paragraph 10 imply that *namaz* is —

   ○ A. a type of bread.
   ○ B. a type of prayer.
   ○ C. a type of building.
   ○ D. a type of bed.

2. A detail that shows they had to travel in secret is —

   ○ A. they had only a little food and water.
   ○ B. they said prayers before leaving.
   ○ C. they performed ablutions quickly in the darkness.
   ○ D. they used sand instead of water to perform ablutions.

3. You can infer that the group stopped every few minutes because —

   ○ A. they needed to hide from guards.
   ○ B. Ahmedi's mother needed to rest and breathe.
   ○ C. they needed to find the correct path.
   ○ D. Ahmedi needed to rest because of her leg.

# Close Read

Reread *The Other Side of the Sky*. As you reread, complete the Skills Focus questions below. Then use your answers and annotations from the questions to help you complete the Write activity.

## ◎ SKILLS FOCUS

1. Identify evidence of how the author uses a chronological text structure. Explain the effect of this structure and how it helps you to understand the author's feelings.

2. Identify evidence that describes the personal characteristics of Ghulam Ali and his wife. How do these descriptions help you better understand them as individuals?

3. Identify clues that tell about the obstacles and hardships that Farah Ahmedi and her mother had to overcome. Then explain what those clues tell you about how the narrator's personal qualities enabled her to survive.

## ✎ WRITE

LITERARY ANALYSIS:  What ideas related to survival during the most challenging times are implied by this excerpt? Write a brief response answering this question. Remember to use evidence from the text to support your response.

Please note that excerpts and passages in the StudySync® library and this workbook are intended as touchstones to generate interest in an author's work. The excerpts and passages do not substitute for the reading of entire texts, and StudySync® strongly recommends that students seek out and purchase the whole literary or informational work in order to experience it as the author intended. Links to online resellers are available in our digital library. In addition, complete works may be ordered through an authorized reseller by filling out and returning to StudySync® the order form enclosed in this workbook.

Reading & Writing Companion    **45**

# The Story of Anniko

FICTION
Charlotte Blake Alston
2000

## Introduction

This adaptation of Molly Melching's French story *Anniko!* is told by storyteller and performer Charlotte Blake Alston. The tale originates from the Wolof language of Senegal, where Melching lived and founded Tostan, a non-profit organization that advocates on behalf of human rights and sustainable development in local communities. Set in a similar village, Anniko's story is one of sudden tragedy and recovery in the welcoming arms of an unexpected community.

# "Anniko uttered a silent prayer before she entered that thick forest."

1   There was once a little girl named Anniko who lived very happily in a village with her mother, father, sisters, and brothers until—one day—a very sad thing began to happen. A sickness came to her village and swept through like an angry fire. No one was spared—except Anniko.

2   Anniko was grief-stricken and lonely, but she knew she could not remain there. Sadly, she began walking away from her village. She walked and walked until she found herself standing at the edge of a thick, thick forest. There were stories of this forest—stories of those who had entered it but had never returned. There were also stories of a village on the other side of that forest where, just as in Anniko's own home, a stranger would be welcomed in. But she would have to enter that thick forest in order to find the path that would lead her to that village.

3   Anniko uttered a silent prayer before she entered that thick forest. She walked and walked, pushing aside wide leaves and long vines. She grew tired, but she continued on. Well, her prayers were answered that day, and she came to the path that would lead her to the village. She followed that path to the other side of the forest.

4   *What a beautiful country this is*, Anniko thought as she walked. Soon the village came into sight and the villagers all came out to greet her. It was then that Anniko noticed that these villagers had one rather **unique characteristic.** They all had long necks with heads that sat at the tops of their necks. Even their babies had long necks with little heads at the top. Anniko had never seen anything like this before.

5   The villagers were about to greet Anniko, but they couldn't believe their eyes. She had a short neck—much like yours and mine. They had never seen anything like this before and they weren't quite sure what to do or say. One of them asked what a little girl like Anniko would be doing in that forest alone. Anniko began to tell all that had happened to her, her family and her village. Something about Anniko made the Longnecks trust her, so they invited her to stay.

6   They were right. Anniko was warm, caring and respectful. She worked, danced and played with the villagers. She **accompanied** the Longnecks to the marketplace and shared in their celebrations and their sorrows. But the thing that was most special about Anniko was that every morning, very early, Anniko would rise and cross the village singing:

Yee si naa leen
Yee si naa leen yen
Yewu nama deyman
Te yee si naa leen itam
Yewu jotnaa
Yee si naa leen
Yee si naa leen yen

which means: *I'm coming to wake you up. I'm up, a new day has begun. I'm coming to wake you also, people.*

7   Singing was very much a part of Anniko's life in her old village but, unbelievable as it might sound, the Longnecks had never heard singing before. They thought this was a wonderful way to be awakened each morning. Soon they would not get up and go about their work until they heard Anniko's sweet song. They loved her even more because of this special gift she brought to them.

8   But in this village—as in all villages in the world—there was one evil, jealous, small-hearted man. He had not liked Anniko from the first day he saw her because she was different. One day he called to her and said, "You do not belong here. You are different from us. You have a—short neck! Differences can only lead to problems in this village. You should take yourself away to avoid bringing trouble here!"

9   The words stung Anniko's heart. Without thinking, she ran off and found herself in the middle of that same thick forest. The rainy season had come so the vines hung longer, the leaves had grown larger, the **foliage** was thicker . . . and Anniko became afraid. She could not even see where she was stepping, so after a while she stopped and rested. Night fell quickly.

10  Early the next morning, all the Longnecks lay in their beds waiting to hear Anniko's sweet song. But there was only silence. One by one, they began to rise from their beds and ask, "Where is Anniko? Have you seen Anniko?" They gathered in the center of the village, and one of the elders said, "I think I know who might know something. Follow me." He led them to the home of that evil, jealous, small-hearted man who told them—almost with pride—how he had spared the village of problems by sending away the different one.

11  The villagers were **furious.** They had to think of a way to help Anniko find her way back. They could not go into the forest because they would become lost themselves. One of Anniko's friends had an idea. She said, "Maybe we can

sing as Anniko has sung to us. Maybe she will hear our voices and that will help her find her way back."

12 Well, not only had the Longnecks never heard singing before Anniko's arrival, they had never tried to sing themselves. They agreed it was important to try. They decided they would sing Anniko's name and tell her they were sad and wanted her back. So they all stood side by side in the center of the village and began to sing for the very first time:

Anniko ni sa wa ni
Anniko ni sa wa ni
Anniko ni sa wa ni
Wo, wo, wo chi ka nay, nay, nay
Wo, wo, wo chi ka nay, nay, nay
Hey, ho bi ci ni
Hey, ho bi ci ni

which means: *Anniko, return quickly. Wo, wo, wo, we are sad without you. Hey, ho, we ask you to return.*

13 They sang and sang, stronger and stronger. Their voices traveled quickly into the forest and reached the place where Anniko sat. When she heard the singing, she knew it was the Longnecks trying to help her find her way home. She followed the sound of the voices to the path that took her into the village once again. The villagers rejoiced when they saw that she was safe with them. They invited her to stay with them as long as she wished.

14 The chief of the village said to Anniko, to the villagers, and to that evil, jealous, small-hearted man: "It is not the length of your neck that is important. It is the goodness of your heart."

From *More Ready-to-Tell Tales from Around the World*, 2005. Used by permission of August House.

### ✏ WRITE

DISCUSSION: "The Story of Anniko" is a folktale from Senegal. Why do you think it's important to read folktales from different cultures and times? What can you learn from reading folktales in addition to studying history and informational texts about these cultures? Write notes to prepare for a discussion of these questions. Use examples from the text as well as other myths and folktales you have read to support your points.

# Icarus and Daedalus

FICTION
Josephine Preston Peabody
1897

## Introduction

In her lifetime, longtime Wellesley professor Josephine Preston Peabody wrote award-winning plays, books of poetry, and also a collection of retellings of Greek mythology. A project perhaps inspired by Nathaniel Hawthorne's *Greek Myths: A Wonder Book for Boys and Girls*, Peabody's *Old Greek Folk Stories Told Anew* added more poetically written tales to those available in the English vernacular, including the miniature tragedy of "Icarus and Daedalus." Daedalus and Icarus, a father and son duo, explore the limits of human ingenuity on their quest for freedom

# "Who could remember to be careful when he was to fly for the first time?"

1   Among all those mortals who grew so wise that they learned the secrets of the gods, none was more **cunning** than Daedalus.

2   He once built, for King Minos of Crete, a wonderful Labyrinth of winding ways so cunningly tangled up and twisted around that, once inside, you could never find your way out again without a magic clue. But the king's favor veered with the wind, and one day he had his master architect imprisoned in a tower. Daedalus managed to escape from his cell; but it seemed impossible to leave the island, since every ship that came or went was well guarded by order of the king.

3   At length, watching the sea-gulls in the air,—the only creatures that were sure of liberty,—he thought of a plan for himself and his young son Icarus, who was captive with him.

4   Little by little, he gathered a store of feathers great and small. He fastened these together with thread, moulded them in with wax, and so fashioned two great wings like those of a bird. When they were done, Daedalus fitted them to his own shoulders, and after one or two efforts, he found that by waving his arms he could winnow the air and **cleave** it, as a swimmer does the sea. He held himself aloft, wavered this way and that with the wind, and at last, like a great fledgling, he learned to fly.

Daedalus made wings for himself and his son, Icarus.

5   Without delay, he fell to work on a pair of wings for the boy Icarus, and taught him carefully how to use them, bidding him beware of **rash** adventures among the stars. "Remember," said the father, "never to fly very low or very high, for the fogs about the earth would weigh you down, but the blaze of the sun will surely melt your feathers apart if you go too near."

Skill:
Setting

*This story is set in Crete during the rule of King Minos. He was in the story of Theseus and the Minotaur. This was around the same time. I can see that Crete is an island, and that explains why Daedalus couldn't just run away.*

**Skill:**
Greek and Latin
Affixes and Roots

*Captivity looks like captive, so the words could have a similar root and meaning. The suffix -ity makes words into nouns, so I bet this word means something like "imprisonment."*

6    For Icarus, these cautions went in at one ear and out by the other. Who could remember to be careful when he was to fly for the first time? Are birds careful? Not they! And not an idea remained in the boy's head but the one joy of escape.

7    The day came, and the fair wind that was to set them free. The father bird put on his wings, and, while the light urged them to be gone, he waited to see that all was well with Icarus, for the two could not fly hand in hand. Up they rose, the boy after his father. The hateful ground of Crete sank beneath them; and the country folk, who caught a glimpse of them when they were high above the tree-tops, took it for a vision of the gods,—Apollo[1], perhaps, with Cupid[2] after him.

8    At first there was a terror in the joy. The wide vacancy of the air dazed them,—a glance downward made their brains reel. But when a great wind filled their wings, and Icarus felt himself sustained, like a halcyon-bird[3] in the hollow of a wave, like a child uplifted by his mother, he forgot everything in the world but joy. He forgot Crete and the other islands that he had passed over: he saw but vaguely that winged thing in the distance before him that was his father Daedalus. He longed for one draught of flight to **quench** the thirst of his captivity: he stretched out his arms to the sky and made towards the highest heavens.

9    Alas for him! Warmer and warmer grew the air. Those arms, that had seemed to uphold him, relaxed. His wings **wavered**, drooped. He fluttered his young hands vainly,—he was falling,—and in that terror he remembered. The heat of the sun had melted the wax from his wings; the feathers were falling, one by one, like snowflakes; and there was none to help.

10    He fell like a leaf tossed down the wind, down, down, with one cry that overtook Daedalus far away. When he returned, and sought high and low for the poor boy, he saw nothing but the bird-like feathers afloat on the water, and he knew that Icarus was drowned.

11    The nearest island he named Icaria, in memory of the child; but he, in heavy grief, went to the temple of Apollo in Sicily, and there hung up his wings as an offering. Never again did he attempt to fly.

---

1. **Apollo** In Greek and Roman mythology, Apollo is the son of Zeus and Leto, and a god of many realms, including music, the sun, poetry, and more.
2. **Cupid** In classical mythology, Cupid is the god of love and attraction.
3. **halcyon-bird** a bird-like figure in Greek mythology with the power to calm the rough ocean waves, symbolizing a sense of peace or tranquility

# First Read

Read "Icarus and Daedalus." After you read, complete the Think Questions below.

## ☁ THINK QUESTIONS

1. What materials were the wings Icarus and Daedalus wore made from? Cite specific evidence from the text to support your answer.

2. What did the country folk who saw the pair flying away from Crete think? Cite specific evidence from the text to support your answer.

3. As Icarus was falling, what did he remember at last? Cite specific evidence from the text to support your answer.

4. Find the word **quench** in paragraph 8 of "Icarus and Daedalus." Use context clues in the surrounding sentences, as well as the sentence in which the word appears, to determine the word's meaning. Write your definition here and identify clues that helped you figure out the meaning.

5. Read the following dictionary entry:

**waver**
wa•ver \'wāvər\
verb
1. to sway or tremble
2. to become weaker

Which definition most closely matches the meaning of *wavered* in paragraph 9? Write the correct definition of *wavered* here and explain how you figured it out.

Please note that excerpts and passages in the StudySync® library and this workbook are intended as touchstones to generate interest in an author's work. The excerpts and passages do not substitute for the reading of entire texts, and StudySync® strongly recommends that students seek out and purchase the whole literary or informational work in order to experience it as the author intended. Links to online resellers are available in our digital library. In addition, complete works may be ordered through an authorized reseller by filling out and returning to StudySync® the order form enclosed in this workbook.

Reading & Writing Companion    53

# Skill: Greek and Latin Affixes and Roots

Use the Checklist to analyze Greek and Latin Affixes and Roots in "Icarus and Daedalus." Refer to the sample student annotations about Greek and Latin Affixes and Roots in the text.

## ••• CHECKLIST FOR GREEK AND LATIN AFFIXES AND ROOTS

In order to identify Greek and Latin affixes and roots, note the following:

- ✓ the root

- ✓ the prefix and/or suffix

To use common, grade-appropriate Greek or Latin affixes and roots as clues to the meaning of a word, use the following questions as a guide:

- ✓ Can I identify the root of this word? Should I look in a dictionary or other resource?

- ✓ What is the meaning of the root?

- ✓ Can I identify the prefix and/or suffix of this word? Should I look in a dictionary or other resource?

- ✓ What is the meaning of the prefix and/or suffix?

- ✓ Does this suffix change the word's part of speech?

- ✓ How do the word parts work together to show the word's meaning and part of speech?

# Skill: Greek and Latin Affixes and Roots

Reread paragraph 8 of "Icarus and Daedalus" and the dictionary entries. Then, using the Checklist on the previous page, answer the multiple-choice questions below.

## ⟳ YOUR TURN

1. **vacancy** va•can•cy \ˈvā-kan-sē\
   **Origin:** from the Latin *vacare* meaning "to be empty"

   Based on its context and root, what is the most likely meaning of *vacancy*?
   - ○ A. vacationing
   - ○ B. being empty
   - ○ C. empty
   - ○ D. emptiness

2. **sustained** sus•tained \sus-ˈtānd\
   **Origin:** From the Latin *sustinere* meaning "keep up, maintain"

   Based on its context and root, what is the most likely meaning of *sustained*?
   - ○ A. held down
   - ○ B. held up
   - ○ C. held out
   - ○ D. extended

3. **vaguely** vague•ly \ˈvāg-lē\
   **Origin**: from the Latin *vagus* meaning "wandering, uncertain" + the adverbial suffix *-ly*

   Based on its context, suffix, and root, what is the most likely meaning of *vaguely*?
   - ○ A. in a wandering way
   - ○ B. uncertain
   - ○ C. uncertainly
   - ○ D. wandering

# SETTING

sync

# Skill:
# Setting

Use the Checklist to analyze Setting in "Icarus and Daedalus." Refer to the sample student annotations about Setting in the text.

### ••• CHECKLIST FOR SETTING

In order to identify how particular elements of a story interact, note the following:

✓ the setting of the story

✓ the characters in the text and the problems they face

✓ how the events of the plot unfold, and how that affects the setting and characters

✓ how the setting shapes the characters and plot

To analyze how particular elements of a story interact, consider the following questions as a guide:

✓ What is the setting(s) of the story?

✓ How does the setting affect the characters and plot?

✓ How does the plot unfold? How does that affect the setting(s)?

✓ How do the characters' decisions affect the plot and setting(s)?

SETTING

Skill:
Setting

Reread paragraphs 8–11 of "Icarus and Daedalus." Then, using the Checklist on the previous page, answer the multiple-choice questions below.

## ↻ YOUR TURN

1. This question has two parts. First, answer Part A. Then, answer Part B.

   **Part A:** The setting of paragraph 8 affects the characters by —

   ○ A. making the characters feel excited to be home.
   ○ B. making the characters feel terrified from the great height.
   ○ C. making the characters feel bitter for being imprisoned for so long.
   ○ D. making the characters feel shock and joy from the wide-open sky.

   **Part B:** Which of the following details BEST supports your response to Part A?

   ○ A. At first there was a terror in the joy. The wide vacancy of the air dazed them.
   ○ B. At first there was a terror in the joy . . . he forgot everything in the world but joy.
   ○ C. . . . he forgot everything in the world but joy . . . he saw but vaguely that winged thing in the distance
   ○ D. He longed for one draught of flight to quench the thirst of his captivity.

2. The setting influences the plot of the story by causing —

   ○ A. Icarus's wings to melt.
   ○ B. Daedalus to lose his way.
   ○ C. King Minos to lose sight of them.
   ○ D. Daedalus and Icarus to become exhausted.

ICARUS AND DAEDALUS

# Close Read

Reread "Icarus and Daedalus." As you reread, complete the Skills Focus questions below. Then use your answers and annotations from the questions to help you complete the Write activity.

## ◎ SKILLS FOCUS

1. Identify descriptions of the setting. Explain how these details affect the characters and plot.

2. Consider the characteristics of Daedalus. Find an event in the story and explain how it is a result of Daedalus's traits.

3. Consider the characteristics of Icarus. Find an event in the story and explain how it is a result of Icarus's traits.

4. In both "The Story of Anniko" and "Icarus and Daedalus," characters flee from a dangerous situation to find themselves in another dangerous situation—but with different outcomes. Identify an event from "Icarus and Daedalus" in which the outcome differs from "The Story of Anniko." Then explain a lesson taught by each text.

5. Identify a detail from "Icarus and Daedalus" that expresses the message or theme, and explain how this theme is meaningful to modern readers.

## ✏ WRITE

COMPARE AND CONTRAST: Write a response comparing and contrasting the settings of "The Story of Anniko" and "Icarus and Daedalus." In your response, explain how the different settings influence characters' actions and plot development. Remember to use evidence from the texts to support your response.

# The New Colossus

POETRY
Emma Lazarus
1883

## Introduction

Emma Lazarus (1849–1887) was a 19th-century American poet best known for her work "The New Colossus," a poetic tribute to the Statue of Liberty. Originally written for a Liberty fundraiser, the poem lay forgotten for almost 20 years before revived interest led to it being engraved on a brass plaque at the base of the statue in 1903. The title of the poem refers to the Colossus of Rhodes, a towering bronze statue of the sun god Helios that was erected in the ancient Greek city of Rhodes to celebrate a military victory over Cyprus. Almost 100 feet high, the Colossus of Rhodes was one of the tallest statues of its time and is now considered

# "Give me your tired, your poor, Your huddled masses yearning to breathe free . . ."

**NOTES**

**Skill: Figurative Language**

The title of the poem is an allusion, or reference, to the Colossus of Rhodes. Referring to ancient Greece adds a sense of importance and grandness. This makes me think both statues are important, even though Lazarus says they are different.

**Skill: Poetic Elements and Structure**

I know that sonnets are emotional poems that are like songs. Lazarus uses emotional language when talking about immigrants, so the form enhances the emotional effect. It's clear that America gave so much hope to so many people.

1   Not like the **brazen** giant of Greek fame,
2   With conquering limbs astride from land to land;
3   Here at our sea-washed, sunset gates shall stand
4   A mighty woman with a torch, whose flame
5   Is the imprisoned lightning, and her name
6   Mother of **Exiles**. From her beacon-hand
7   Glows world-wide welcome; her mild eyes command
8   The air-bridged harbor that twin cities frame.

9   "Keep, ancient lands, your storied **pomp**!" cries she
10  With silent lips. "Give me your tired, your poor,
11  Your huddled masses yearning to breathe free,
12  The **wretched refuse** of your teeming shore.
13  Send these, the homeless, tempest-tost to me,
14  I lift my lamp beside the golden door!"

Illustration of immigrants arriving in New York City and seeing the Statue of Liberty, 1887

From THE NEW COLOSSUS by Emma Lazarus, Copyright ©2014.

# First Read

Read "The New Colossus." After you read, complete the Think Questions below.

## ☁ THINK QUESTIONS

1. The title of the poem refers to the Colossus of Rhodes—a giant statue of the sun god, Helios— erected in the ancient Greek city of Rhodes to celebrate the city's victory over Cyprus. How do you know from the poem that the "mighty woman with a torch" is also a statue? Cite textual evidence to support your understanding.

2. Who is the "mighty woman with a torch" not like? How is she different? Cite textual evidence to support your answer.

3. To whom is the "mighty woman with a torch" offering a "world-wide welcome"? Cite specific evidence from the poem to support your answer.

4. Find the word **brazen** in the first line of "The New Colossus." Use context clues in the surrounding words, as well as the line in which the word appears, to determine the word's meaning. Write your definition here and identify clues that helped you figure out the meaning.

5. Use context clues to determine the meaning of **exiles** as it is used in line 6 of "The New Colossus." Write your definition here and identify clues that helped you figure out the meaning. Then check the meaning in a dictionary.

Please note that excerpts and passages in the StudySync® library and this workbook are intended as touchstones to generate interest in an author's work. The excerpts and passages do not substitute for the reading of entire texts, and StudySync® strongly recommends that students seek out and purchase the whole literary or informational work in order to experience it as the author intended. Links to online resellers are available in our digital library. In addition, complete works may be ordered through an authorized reseller by filling out and returning to StudySync® the order form enclosed in this workbook.

Reading & Writing Companion

61

# Skill: Poetic Elements and Structure

Use the Checklist to analyze Poetic Elements and Structure in "The New Colossus." Refer to the sample student annotations about Poetic Elements and Structure in the text.

## ••• CHECKLIST FOR POETIC ELEMENTS AND STRUCTURE

In order to identify poetic elements and structure, note the following:

✓ the form and overall structure of the poem, such as:

- sonnet: a poem with 14 lines broken into two stanzas, with a set rhyme scheme and a set meter

✓ the rhyme, rhythm, and meter, if present

✓ other sound elements, such as:

- alliteration: the repetition of initial consonant sounds, as with the *s* sound in "Cindy sweeps the sand"

✓ lines and stanzas in the poem that suggest its meaning

✓ ways that the poem's form or structure connects to the poem's meaning

To analyze how a poem's form or structure contributes to its meaning, consider the following questions:

✓ What poetic form does the poet use? What is the structure?

✓ How do the lines and stanzas and their lengths affect the meaning?

✓ How do the form and structure contribute to the poem's meaning?

# Skill: Poetic Elements and Structure

Reread lines 9–14 of "The New Colossus." Then, using the Checklist on the previous page, answer the multiple-choice questions below.

## 🔄 YOUR TURN

1. This question has two parts. First, answer Part A. Then, answer Part B.

   **Part A:** Think about the meaning of the stanza and the effect that the rhyme scheme has on it. What message is expressed in the stanza?

   - A. People around the world are in pain.
   - B. The statue stands silent.
   - C. There is freedom for all in the United States of America.
   - D. Many people are huddled in masses.

   **Part B:** Which set of rhyming lines best supports your answer to Part A?

   - A. "'Keep, ancient lands, your storied pomp!' cries she." / "'Send these, the homeless, tempest-tost to me'"
   - B. "'Your huddled masses yearning to breathe free,'" / "'Send these, the homeless, tempest-tost to me'"
   - C. "'The wretched refuse of your teeming shore.'" / "'Send these, the homeless, tempest-tost to me'"
   - D. "With silent lips. 'Give me your tired, your poor,'" / "'The wretched refuse of your teeming shore.'"

# Skill:
# Figurative Language

Use the Checklist to analyze Figurative Language in "The New Colossus." Refer to the sample student annotations about Figurative Language in the text.

## ••• CHECKLIST FOR FIGURATIVE LANGUAGE

To determine the meanings of figures of speech in a text, note the following:

✓ words that mean one thing literally and suggest something else

✓ similes, such as "strong as an ox"

✓ metaphors, such as "her eyes were stars"

✓ allusions, or indirect references to people, texts, events, or ideas, such as

- saying of a setting, "the place was a Garden of Eden" (Biblical allusion)

- saying of a character whose snooping caused problems, "he opened a Pandora's box" (allusion to mythology)

- calling someone who likes romance "a real Romeo" (allusion to Shakespeare)

✓ other language in the text used in a nonliteral way

In order to interpret the meaning of a figure of speech in context, ask the following questions:

✓ Does any of the descriptive language in the text compare two seemingly unlike things?

✓ Do any descriptions include *like* or *as* to indicate a simile?

✓ Is there a direct comparison that suggests a metaphor?

✓ What literary, Biblical, or mythological allusions do you recognize?

✓ How does the use of this figure of speech change your understanding of the thing or person being described?

In order to analyze the impact of figurative language on the meaning of a text, use the following questions as a guide:

✓ Where does figurative language appear in the text? What does it mean?

✓ Why does the author use figurative language rather than literal language?

# Skill:
# Figurative Language

Reread lines 9–14 of "The New Colossus." Then, using the Checklist on the previous page, answer the multiple-choice questions below.

## ⟳ YOUR TURN

1. This question has two parts. First, answer Part A. Then, answer Part B.

   **Part A:** Which of the lines uses figurative language to best convey the message that the United States is a land of opportunity?

   ○ A. "'Keep, ancient lands, your storied pomp!' cries she"
   ○ B. "'I lift my lamp beside the golden door!'"
   ○ C. "'The wretched refuse of your teeming shore.'"
   ○ D. "'Send these, the homeless, tempest-tost to me'"

   **Part B:** Which of the following best explains how the figure of speech you chose in Part A conveys the message of American opportunity?

   ○ A. The phrase "storied pomp" refers to the riches, which the immigrants may gain by coming to the United States.
   ○ B. The phrase "golden door" conveys the message of American opportunity because it suggests both a precious metal and something opening.
   ○ C. In "wretched refuse" and "teeming shore," Lazarus explains the poverty that motivated many immigrants to come to the United States.
   ○ D. By calling the immigrants "homeless" and "tempest-tost," the poet emphasizes the misery and danger they are leaving behind for new opportunity in the United States.

Please note that excerpts and passages in the StudySync® library and this workbook are intended as touchstones to generate interest in an author's work. The excerpts and passages do not substitute for the reading of entire texts, and StudySync® strongly recommends that students seek out and purchase the whole literary or informational work in order to experience it as the author intended. Links to online resellers are available in our digital library. In addition, complete works may be ordered through an authorized reseller by filling out and returning to StudySync® the order form enclosed in this workbook.

Reading & Writing Companion  65

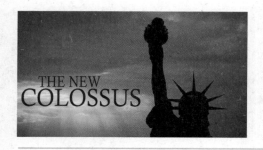

# Close Read

Reread "The New Colossus." As you reread, complete the Skills Focus questions below. Then use your answers and annotations from the questions to help you complete the Write activity.

## ◎ SKILLS FOCUS

1. "Sea-washed, sunset gates" is a metaphor used in line 3. What might this metaphor mean in the context of the poem? What does it suggest about the poem's deeper meaning or message? How does it affect the poem's tone?

2. Highlight evidence in the last six lines that "The New Colossus" is a sonnet. What is the effect of this structure? Explain your answer using evidence from the text.

3. Emma Lazarus uses an allusion to the Colossus of Rhodes in her poem. What is the effect of this allusion? What is her deeper message about America and its values? Explain your reasoning with evidence from the text.

4. Recall that a tempest is a violent and windy storm. In the poem, it is used in a figurative sense. Highlight its use in line 13. Given the poem's message, how might Lazarus be using "tempest-tost" here?

5. Why do you think we still read this poem about the Statue of Liberty? Why are its themes and message still relevant to people in America today? Explain your answer using evidence from the text.

## ✏ WRITE

LITERARY ANALYSIS: What does Emma Lazarus want readers to know about the United States? What is the poem's deeper message or theme about America? Use your understanding of figurative language and poetic structure and elements to determine her message.

# The Third Elevator

FICTION
Aimee Bender
2009

## Introduction

Aimee Bender (b. 1969) is an acclaimed American author known for her distinctive magical realist style. To this end, "The Third Elevator" is a classic Aimee Bender story, bringing together the author's signature wit, melancholy, and whimsy, and setting it in a world of make-believe. In this particular world, there is a rigid order wherein loggers, miners, and royalty are kept separate by three distinct elevators. When two birds of different feathers mate and hatch a mysterious egg, a cloud is released into the air and begins to make inhabitants of the kingdom question just which of the existing boundaries are set in stone.

# "One was made of gold, one was made of wood, and the third was made entirely of feathers."

NOTES

1   The queen took a swan for her pet. The bird was white and large, with a body so puffed out and fluffy it looked just like a small cloud, only with legs, with a beak, and with bright beaded black eyes.

2   "Throw him up in the air," said the queen, "and who knows who we'd fool."

3   But this swan had moods that were heavy. His disposition was not cloud-like at all. He took the world very seriously and sometimes had a hard time because of that. He didn't even like to fly. He preferred swimming instead and, occasionally, would take a dip in the moat, leaving bright white feathers in his trail like the opposite of footprints. To keep her pet company the queen spent much of her day with the swan, and they walked around the castle grounds together. The two were fine companions and the queen respected the swan's sad moods, but she did worry about her pet and wished she could find him a proper mate. She made an effort to introduce him to other, sexy swans, but the queen's swan always arched to the side and refused to interlock his neck with theirs. He was picky. He preferred, in general, to tour the moat.

Skill:
Character

*The narrator describes the birds like people. They walk around, have conversations, laugh, and fall in love. I think they'll be important in the story because they are so much like humans. I wonder if their relationship will affect the conflict of the story?*

4   However, on his own time, while the queen was in the castle hearing citizens complain to her crowned head, the swan liked to go visit with the bluebirds who were scattered throughout the royal hedge like huge loud blueberries. The bluebirds were a lively bunch and, on occasion, came out to visit with the royal swan. Once, on a Wednesday, a bluebird runt hopped out, tiny and cobalt[1], and she jumped over to the swan and leapt onto his white lush back.

5   The swan started nervously, but the bluebird insisted that she would not get off the swan's back until they spent the day together. The two strolled around the gardens, discussing flight and seed and feather rot, and the bluebird was very funny and kept the swan laughing his deep trumpeting laugh. It was a beautiful, rich sound, and one that wasn't often heard on the palace grounds. The birds even toured the moat together, the bluebird chattering the whole time. By the end of the day, they were deeply in love.

1. **cobalt** a deep blue pigment

6   So the swan, being highly educated as most royal pets are, went straight to his mistress who was tired and sweaty after listening to complaint after complaint, and wrote a document with fancy ink on thick cream-colored paper declaring that he and the runt bluebird wished to be married. The queen, while having her shoulders massaged, read the note and put down one daintily booted foot.

7   "I don't think so," she said. "You are a royal bird and ought to marry something more—"

8   The bluebird, still nestled like a lapis lazuli[2] necklace on the swan's puffy back, tilted her head.

9   The queen winced. "I mean, you ought to marry something else—" she continued.

10  The swan hung his long white neck and the bluebird flew into the queen's eye. She did not peck it out, but just placed the cold hard cartilage triangle of her beak next to the liquidy white of the queen's tear duct.

11  "Bless you both," said the queen meekly.

* * *

12  The swan said he would not leave his mistress, so the two birds stayed close by, setting up a home just outside the palace grounds where the little bluebird made a nest large enough for the both of them. They were living contentedly in it, getting to know each other, and after a few weeks the runt bluebird laid an unusual egg. It was half the size of her body, and speckled. The **mollified** queen came over and praised its size and shape. The swan paced back and forth.

13  "What will it look like?" he asked the queen. "What if it's moody and depressed like I have been? What if it's a freak bird?"

14  The queen tried to comfort her pet but the swan just paced more. All the citizens of the kingdom were curious, and the egg was the topic of many discussions and debates at the local tavern for weeks. The bluebird chattered and sat in the nest patiently, and the swan brought her seeds and twigs and stroked down her feathers. He told her his worries. She thought they were funny.

15  When the egg finally opened, to the surprise of everyone, it revealed nothing but a cloud, pale blue in color, rising slowly in the air. The queen's mouth dropped open. The bluebird trilled with laughter. The swan, with a proud and

2. **lapis lazuli**  a blue metamorphic rock, used in jewelry and for decoration

powerful ache in his breast, watched in awe as his child gained altitude, higher and higher, until the cloud lifted up enough to float gently to the next county, the wind hovering beneath it like the sweetest of cradles.

\* \* \*

16    About two miles from the swan's nest was a glass-walled lobby unattached to any building. It stood smack in the center of the kingdom and had for as long as anyone could remember. Inside this lobby were three elevators. One was made of gold, one was made of wood, and the third was made entirely of feathers.

17    The gold elevator would descend ten stories down, down down down, into the middle of the earth. There, it opened its doors to a mineshaft where workers stuck shovels into the walls and picked and pulled until nuggets of gold fell onto their feet. Then they put the gold into the gold elevator. The elevator closed its doors on its own accord when it reached its weight requirement, and a collection agency came and collected the goods once daily. No miners were allowed to get inside the elevator and ride on up to the fresher air of the lobby, the elucidation of sunlight.

18    The elevator made of wood stayed on ground level and had a set of gnarled bark doors at both ends. One set opened to the lobby and the other opened to the muted light of a forest, thick with trees and thickets, flickering with broken lemon-yellow rays. Here, the loggers who were making timber from trees would take their stacks of chopped-up trunks and place them in careful rows inside the wood elevator. The forest was quiet, the ground soft with moss, and the loggers would whistle tunes their mothers had sung to them long ago, when they were as small as the smallest sapling. Now their arms were solid, muscles hard inside skin. They loaded the wood elevator until it was heavy enough, and then its bark doors shut slowly, smelling of resin, and re-opened, on the other side, to the lobby. The loggers returned to chopping and felling and whistling.

19    The feather elevator went forty-five stories high, up on its metal pole, the lightest elevator ever made. Birds eyed its slow **ascent** suspiciously but assumed it was a large rectangular bird, for it smelled like them and even fluttered slightly. But where was the beak? At the forty-fifth floor, the elevator opened its light grayish doors and let the air inside. It could rotate around on its pole there, hoping to catch something in the upper stratosphere. Sometimes curious birds would dart inside its open mouth, sticking old twigs and more feathers inside it, and then the elevator would close up, descend to the lobby, open its doors, and reveal nothing more than scraggle. But once, the elevator descended its forty-five floors, and arrived exactly on time with the other two. At the count of three, from the gold spilled gold, from the wood

NOTES

tumbled fine logs, and when the feather elevator opened its doors, out drifted one pale blue cloud.

\* \* \*

20    On the other side of the kingdom, touring the moat as usual, the melancholy swan heard word of the caught cloud. He'd never even been to the famous elevators that held up the local economy, operated on their own schedules, and were visited once daily by the gold and timber collectors, but the following afternoon, he waddled over. Unimpressed by the gold and wood, he went directly to the elevator of feathers and stepped inside. He spoke in hushed tones to its walls, whispering to the old shed bones of his friends, persuading it to go high, in the hopes that he would see and catch his own. He felt nervous rising inside the closed box, having never been in such a small space before, but when the doors opened he stood at the edge and trumpeted into the sky for hours, hoping against hope, putting his whole longing into his voice: *Come see me, child, come see me.* Then, just as the sun was starting a long descent, his pale blue offspring came floating by. The swan's heart leapt. Luckily, the wind on this day was just so, and the swan was able to get the cloud back inside the small rectangular elevator with him. The doors shut, and they rode down the forty-five flights together. The swan asked his child polite questions, but the cloud was silent, just floating there in that room of feathers. When they hit ground level, the two did not exit. The swan wasn't entirely sure what to do, what would be a fatherly act, but, following his instinct, he held out his enormous wings and invited the cloud to gather underneath them. There the two huddled, puffy pale feathers against puffy pale atmosphere, until the cloud began to diffuse from the heat, and then the swan ordered the elevator to begin its rise upstairs, which it did, because birds listen to birds, up and up and up. The doors opened to a sky fading to darker blue, and the swan kissed his child and wished it well, promising to return as soon as possible. The cloud floated away from beneath the wings of its father, drifting into the slow-turning black night. The swan decided not to ride the forty-five floors down, and took off out the doors the second before they shut, wingspan as long as a tree trunk, tears in his snapping black bird eyes, the underside of his wing warm and empty.

\* \* \*

21    One of the loggers was a troublesome logger. He kept his axe very sharp and cut everything down except for trees. He felled telephone poles and even got through cement light posts; he chopped down fire hydrants and trellises but he didn't want to cut down the trees because, he said, they were growing. "Why would I do that?" he told everyone else.

Skill:
Character

*The narrator tells us right away that the logger is "troublesome." He is skilled, but he doesn't want to cut down trees because they are "growing." This seems to be a pretty clear conflict, because loggers are supposed to cut down trees. His question "Why would I do that?" reveals a really kind personality and shows that his attitude toward trees is totally different from everyone else's.*

NOTES

22  The other loggers found him snobbish. "Just cut the trees," they told him, "come on."

23  But the troublesome logger couldn't. He said every time he put the blade of his axe against the bark of a new tree and prepared to slice in, he felt a clanging in his chest and knew if he cut it down he would have a heart attack at that exact same moment.

24  The other loggers then found him **melodramatic.** "Oh go see the boss," they said. "We don't need all these broken telephone poles and, besides, everyone in the kingdom is angry because they can't call each other up."

25  The logger twitched when he heard that. He didn't like to unconnect people. He'd even tried to help the telephone electrical crew but they just yelled at him to stop messing with the wires, and he felt so **agitated** by their yelling at him that he went and cut down a few more telephone poles about a mile away.

26  The boss logger heard about the troublesome logger and called him into his office the next morning. "Son," he said. "I hear you are unable to cut down trees. You must not be a logger at heart. Your father was a fine logger and his father before him was a fine logger but if you are not a logger at heart then we need to get you out of here."

27  The troublesome logger hung his head. His father had been the finest logger ever known, winning speed awards yearly, filling the elevator so early they often took the day off and went hiking up the trails to look for mountain goats. In fact, when he, the best logger's son, had been old enough to become a logger himself, there was a party to initiate him because his genetic logging legacy was so superior to that of the average man. When he'd cut down his first tree, a small elm, they had popped open a bottle of champagne to mark the spot, cream-colored froth pouring over the stump. The young logger, thirteen at the time, had to sit down because his heart was hurting so badly at the sight of the baby elm on its side, leaves dusting the ground, and he perched on the tiny stump, wet with champagne, while his father made constant toasts and got roaringly drunk.

28  Since then, his father had died in his bed, with loggers surrounding him, holding his hands and looking at him with love. As he closed his eyes for the last time, they all leaned in, like a group of trees, and the wind from the window rustled through their arms. His son sat outside on yet another stump, running his palm over the rings.

29  The young logger looked at the boss and agreed that he was wrong for the job. He said he needed to leave but didn't know where to go.

Copyright © BookheadEd Learning, LLC

30   "Well," the boss said, "there's always the mine. They're always looking for good men in the mine."

31   So the logger left the forest of trees he loved and, holding his axe across his chest like a banner, entered the gold elevator and took it ten floors down. The miners were so used to each other they were very surprised to see a new face emerge from the elevator and found the new organization of features disturbing just because it was new.

32   "I'm a former logger," said the logger. "I would like a job here with you. I can dig for gold."

33   The miners jeered at him. "But we don't like loggers," they said.

34   "Please," pleaded the logger.

35   The head miner shrugged and said they always could use extra help. He asked the logger a few questions about **claustrophobia** and then gave him a corner of the cave to work on and told him the best way to get along in the mine was to play poker after dinner and lose. The logger nodded, still clutching his axe. "You won't need that," said the mining boss. The logger clung to it and asked if he could keep it. "I am attached to my axe," he said. The miner handed over a shovel. "Very well," he said. "Just get to work."

36   So the logger began picking apart the wall of the mine. The miners were singing songs—different than the songs the loggers sang—miner songs were in minor keys[3] and tended to be less storytelling-oriented and more repetitive. The logger listened and picked at the wall and hummed along when he thought he'd got the melody down, and then when he hit a chunk of gold in the wall he knocked it out and threw it behind him in the pile.

37   And then felt awful. It was the same feeling he'd had about the tree, a clutching in his chest, at the gold being ripped from the wall and going off into the world to wind up on the wrist of some person somewhere. He doubled over with pain.

38   The miners kept singing.

39   The logger took some deep breaths and then picked up his shovel and began digging at the wall again, with less vigor now, and soon he hit another nugget of gold. He held it, a chip the size of a tooth, and stuck it in his mouth. It fizzed on his tongue. Unable to throw it behind him, he replaced the nugget

---

3. **minor keys** musical scales with note patterns that are sometimes said to produce sadder or more mournful melodies

in the wall and spent some time shoring it back up. Then he picked out a piece of the black wall instead and threw that into the gold pile. He did that for five hours, throwing nuggets of wall into the gold pile, and hiding the nuggets of gold deeper into the wall, and when the boss came around to load up the gold elevator his yell was heard echoing throughout the cave for five minutes after he'd yelled it.

40    "What in the—?" he bellowed.

41    No one answered. The song stopped abruptly in the middle of the counterpoint third round about mountains. Several miners who were eating dinner put down their salami sandwiches nervously. There was not much yelling in the mine due to that echo.

42    The boss toured the miners' faces and when he arrived at the new-miner-former-logger he looked at him and the logger began trembling and stuttering, and the miner just pointed to the elevator and the logger picked up his axe and went back inside. He rode up with the pieces of gold, then walked straight through the wood elevator, and returned to the forest where the trees leaned away from him in the wind.

43    There is no place for me, he thought.

44    He was so agitated he couldn't sleep, so before he went to bed he walked toward a cluster of houses and chopped down two light posts and a mailbox, and curled himself up there on the ground to rest, surrounded by a fanned display of spilled letters.

* * *

45    One of the miners, who regularly filled up the gold elevator and was considered one of the best workers, had watched the logger go up the elevator with curiosity and envy. He hadn't known a person could take that trip.

46    He'd been growing short of breath lately. So, a few hours after the logger had left, the miner told his workmates that he was going to follow that logger and get in the elevator when half the load was full because he had to see the top of the earth again or he was going to die of claustrophobia of the lungs. The miners were a supportive team, because they had to be or they'd all be dead, and so they let him hop inside the gold elevator right before it went up, watching the doors close over his nervous face, cheeks reflecting the piles of metal as if he'd been working for years in sunshine.

47    The doors opened up to that same small lobby, with the two other elevators opening at the same time. Gold spilled onto the ground, and so did the miner.

There were no other humans visible. No sign of that vagabond logger. The miner stepped forward, squinting from the brightness of the glare even though it was early evening—five pm—and the sunlight was cool and lazy. Since he was an honest man, he did not take a nugget of gold but walked out the glass side doors of the lobby, strolling into the surrounding forest. Nearby, he could hear the melodic whistling of the loggers but saw none of them. He breathed in the oxygen thickly, heady from it, and settled himself under a tree. The wood smelled like heaven to the miner, so warm and rich with sun, and he ate some nuts from his pocket and then fell asleep, in oxygenated air, for the first time in over twenty years.

48 The loggers found him as they moved to that part of the forest. It was immediately clear that he wasn't a logger, being that he was covered with tiny black and gold specks from the mine, and so they hauled him, sound asleep, into the elevator with their stacks of wood. He woke up in the lobby again, amidst a pile of timber and lumber.

49 The sun was brighter now and he squinted helplessly at the light. He was hoping to spot the logger from the mine as a guide, but there was no sign of him anywhere. The miner rubbed his eyes. He wasn't sure where to go, so he decided to take the one elevator he hadn't been in up. Up and up and up. He huddled close to the walls. It had been a long time since he'd experienced anything unexpected and he wasn't familiar with this constant rising motion and his heart kept bumping against his throat.

50 When the feather doors opened to sky, the opposite of his life until now, as if he were face to face with the sun, the miner forgot to breathe; he stood there, with the clouds and the birds and the air, speechless. Amen to the firmament, his arms full to the rim of it. Birds—he'd forgotten all about birds!—flew by at face level, wings steady, and the miner laughed out loud at those amazing wingspans. He dazzled his eyes with the brightness of the blue, tears streaming down his cheeks as he clung to those warm feather walls. Who knew there was this kind of ridiculous beauty, just a quarter mile above the mine? He thought of his men, his favorites, fifty-five stories below in darkness, taking chunks out of the earth so that people could decorate their wrists and necks and ankles and fingers.

51 He had to tell them. He had to bring them there, one by one, up to the sky. He wanted them to feel how he felt, to see the birds in such detail, the flash of beaks; he wanted them to breathe in the silver of this gourmet air. After another twenty glorious minutes, and a full rotational view, the elevator went down. The miner hopped out and waited at the gold elevator patiently, and when it opened, full of gold as always, he jumped in it and sank those ten floors. There were his friends, exactly as before, still in the black mining hole, still surrounded by nuggets of gold, a couple of them eating those premade

salami sandwiches bought from the miners' restaurant deeper inside the cave. They looked a little surprised to see their adventurous friend again.

52    "Come with me," said the miner. "You'll never guess how incredible it is. You will never guess what is up there."

53    They all wanted to know before they came. The miner wouldn't tell. All he said was how beautiful it was. He couldn't stop babbling. "Come up," he said, wiping his eyes.

54    No one wanted to.

55    "It's cold up there," said one.

56    "I'm beat," said another miner, curling up in his space on the floor with his gold-dusted pillow and book.

57    "It's incredible," said the adventurous miner. "I must show you. Come with me. Come now."

58    "Tell us," said the other miners. "Then maybe."

59    So the adventurous miner sat down and told of the forest smell of dampness and the crisp air and photosynthesis, and then he told of the feather elevator and the ascent into the sky and the air again, how it was singing air like they'd never breathed before, how the birds' wings were so close he could've touched one with a careful finger and how the feathers would remind them what the word *soft* meant.

60    They listened and nodded but after all that, only one other miner said he felt like going right then. The others had plans to play poker, seven card stud. They said they liked the description and thanked him but explained that they wanted to get a good night's sleep after the game. The miner went and shook them by the shoulders but they still said no, hey, really, thanks anyway. He banged his fist on the rocky wall, which drew blood, but the poker dealer still began shuffling, and the players divvied up the chips, carefully cut from the wall, and after a few more stunned minutes he took the younger fellow with him in the elevator, ten floors up, into the lobby.

61    "You're the only smart one in there," he said, blotting his bloody fist on his pant leg.

62    "I'm real bad at poker," admitted the younger man.

63    Both miners were relieved by the cool night light that was filling the lobby now that the sun was down. The miner wanted to show his friend everything

but he wanted to go to the best part first and so they went straight to the feather elevator and the doors opened and they stepped inside. As soon as their feet were in, the doors shut and it began to rise again, forty-five floors up. The miners held on to each others' shoulders.

64 "I believe I'm afraid of heights," the younger one said.

65 The adventurous miner squeezed the shoulder of his friend. "It's worth it," he said.

66 The elevator smelled of birdseed. The miner put his cheek close to the feathers. The younger miner was starting to hyperventilate from the endless rising and rising, when, finally, the elevator steadied to a stop.

67 "Ready?" said the first.

68 His friend nodded weakly, holding his stomach. The doors opened.

69 The sky was nearly black by now, with stars poking out in tiny white glittering dots. The moon gleamed at half. The adventurous miner had not seen night in those same twenty years. His whole skin bumped up. He felt he should bow but he didn't want to lower his head; he wanted to keep looking and breathing and looking.

70 After a few minutes, he glanced at his younger friend, jittery with the nervousness that comes from sharing something deeply precious. The air was filling him up. He was tempted to try to fly.

71 "Well," he said, unable to keep his voice casual. "So what do you think?"

72 His friend was scratching his head. His breathing had regulated but he looked puzzled.

73 "But it's just like the cave," he said then, pointing to the stars. "Just a whole lot bigger, and it has silver, not gold. I wouldn't want to be a miner here," he said. "It would take such a long long shovel."

74 The adventurous miner was taking so many deep breaths he was starting to get dizzy himself.

75 "It's no cave," he said. "Don't say that."

76 His friend shrugged. "Looks just like the cave to me," he said. "Doesn't feel high at all." He sat at the edge of the box and dangled his legs. The miner crossed his arms. When he spoke, his voice trembled. "I'm showing you the

whole night sky," he said, eyes filling, "and all you have to say for it is that it looks like the cave?"

77   The younger miner didn't look around. The elevator was rotating, very slowly.

78   "See," he said, pointing. "If we got that thing," he said, pointing at the moon which was just coming into their frame of vision, "that would fill up the elevator in one day. Now that would be an easy day."

79   The older miner's head was spinning. He thought quite honestly of pushing the man off the elevator with his foot, kicking him into the air, this man he had spent the last twenty years working with, side by side, gone, in a slim fall.

80   Two swans flew by, bodies lit like opals[4] against the moonlight. The older miner watched their long wings and started to cry.

81   "I've spent my whole life down there," he said.

82   The other man was asleep. When they descended, the miner lugged him out of the feather elevator and stuffed him back in the gold one. The doors shut and down he went. But he himself stayed in the lobby. He slept a long night there on the tiled floor, face pressed to the glass, knees pulled in, a heavy spool unravelling in his chest. He woke only once, in the middle of the night, to notice the swan settled next to him, wings tucked up.

* * *

83   The cloud nestled close to its father. By this point it was confused. It had taken so many trips with the swan down the elevator that it thought it belonged on the ground as well, and spent hours floating one inch above dirt level, **amiable** beside its paternal line.

84   That night it slept beside the man and the bird: buoyant, earthbound.

85   The swan woke up, slightly nervous, because his child was thinning and dissipating and no longer had the robust look of a healthy cloud; his child now looked vague and closer to the curtainy veil of stratus than its usual bouncy alto cumulus self.

86   "Child," he said in the middle of the night, in a low voice so as not to wake the sleeping man next to him with the glowing face, "I think you should go back up and stay there for a while. You belong higher in the atmosphere. I will look at you from down here with such pride and joy," he said.

---

4. **opals** gemstones showing many small points of shifting color against a pale or dark hue

87    The cloud didn't talk but moved one inch closer to the swan's side.

88    The swan repeated himself. The cloud moved closer. The swan stood and took the cloud up with him back to the forty-fifth floor and there they looked out to the world at sunrise, turning lighter and more colorful with each minute, each shade emerging from the darkness, blue first, then green, red last and brightest of all. Applause. The swan asked the cloud to go back out into the air. The cloud didn't move. The swan tried to shove it out, but it is impossible to shove a cloud.

89    Finally they took the elevator back down, forty-five stories. The cloud was spreading into a fog now. The swan picked at the feathers around his breastbone. It was still early morning and the glowing miner was asleep, still glowing. There was a knock on the glass of the lobby and the swan saw his wife, the bluebird. She skipped inside, kissed the vast area of her firstborn, and told her husband she'd laid another egg.

90    The swan blinked, surprised. She said this egg was different—very large and pale green. "What do you think it'll be?" he asked the bluebird nervously, tendrils of cloud swirling on his back. She shrugged her little winged shoulders. "A bird?" she said.

\* \* \*

91    In the morning, all the letters had blown away except one with a return address that read: *King and Queen* on the first line and *Palace* on the second. The logger, still tired and ill, cleared his eyes, and opened the letter. On gold-embossed stationery, it read:

92    *Dear Citizen:*

93    *I am pleased to say you have been selected to be one of the palace courtiers. Please show up at work on Tuesday at eight am sharp and you need not bring anything except this letter, in fact, please don't.*

94    The logger held the letter to his nose. It smelled like flowers and, when he looked closer, he saw that the paper itself was made from hammered-down gardenias, dried into paper stiffness, the smell still caught inside in an olfactory photograph.

95    So the logger showed up on Tuesday at the palace door, which was huge and had no handles, and when he was ushered in he said he was a new courtier and they asked to see the letter and he showed it and then everyone nodded solemnly. "Welcome," said the man with the voice so deep it reverberated in the logger's ribcage. They tried to take away his axe. He

refused. "Sometimes," he explained, "I need to cut things down." They murmured for a while and checked with several levels of authority and then said okay. "But if you get *anywhere* near the king or queen's neck with that," they said, in unison, "we will bomb you to oblivion."

96   The logger nodded, meekly.

97   They sent him to the kitchen to make turtle soup. The kitchen was a huge brassy room with hanging copper pots and pans and piles of white linen tablecloths and a chef with a curling red mustache. The logger was placed at the stove, near a line of sleeping turtles. His job was to pick up each turtle and stick it into a cauldron of boiling water, because the king had requested turtle soup. As might be expected, the logger could not do it. The minute he put the first sleeping turtle in the water and thought he heard a squeak of death so sharp it made his blood curdle into sleet, he fell down, axe and all, and the one turtle boiled and the chef's assistants had to leave their chopping to the chef's annoyance and take the new guy down to the infirmary. There, the nurses were doves and fluttered around, checking his temperature.

98   "I can do no job," the logger said to the air. "I can touch nothing."

99   The doves, eleven in total, nestled into his neck, cooing and soft as breasts, a curved warmth against his carotid artery. He slept like that, and when he woke up he felt much better, renewed, and he sent a prayer up to the dead turtle and his heart seemed to be working steadily, but when he swung his legs out of bed and got ready to go back into the world to find his ever-elusive fate, he discovered that his axe had disappeared.

100   And all the doves were gone. The infirmary was empty. It was perfectly clean and organized and tidy but nothing alive except for him was in it.

101   He busted out the infirmary door into the hallway.

102   "Excuse me?" he said. "Nurse?"

103   The hallway was silent. The carpet was a rich purple and the candles hanging from the walls were dripping elongated beaded tiers of ivory wax.

104   The logger began to panic.

105   He spied a purple-carpeted stairway at the end of the hall and rushed up several flights until he reached a door embossed with gold and he didn't even read the lettering but just charged right on through. These were the chambers of the royal barber, and, inside, the king was sitting on a white chair, covered in a white apron, having his white hair cut.

106 "Have you seen my axe?" cried the logger.

107 The king looked embarrassed. The barber's scissors glinted in the light, encrusted with sapphires. On the floor in the distance the logger spotted a couple of fat rats.

108 "Who is this?" the king asked his nearby courtiers. "You know I don't like to be watched by strangers when my hair is being cut."

109 They had no idea who it was.

110 "I was in the infirmary," said the logger. "Have you seen the doves? I was a courtier for an hour," he said. "But I couldn't cook the turtles for the turtle soup. I need my axe. Where are those doves?"

111 The courtiers, in a group, shrugged. The one with the severe eyebrows looked guiltily at the logger because she knew those doves tended to cause a fair amount of trouble at the infirmary. They were great nurses in daylight but at night seemed to have a problem with kleptomania. She explained this to the logger whose face blanched paler each minute.

112 "Where can I find them?" he said.

113 "They do enjoy riding that feather elevator?" she said.

114 The king, patient up until now because the barber had been cutting some bangs, opened his mouth and ordered the young man out. "Just for that," he bellowed, "I would like MORE turtle soup tonight. Vats and vats of turtle soup!" He was in a bad mood. His wife's good friend the swan had been gone for weeks and she was moody and he couldn't comfort her, and now the barber had just cut one side of his hair too short; the barber'd been distracted by starting to tell his own story of being in the infirmary and getting his fingernail stolen by the doves, so daintily he had not even noticed until he raised his finger up to nibble on the nail and found there was nothing there but skin.

115 "It was very gross," he said now.

116 But no one was listening. The logger was being shoved out by the courtiers through the front door of the palace into the daytime. There, he faced the kingdom for the first time without his axe. He felt small, and odd. He walked, both arms free, all the way to the glass lobby, and stood trembling by the third elevator.

117 There was no button, so he just waited. Everything around him seemed dizzyingly tall. The outside doors of the elevator smelled musty and the feathers were graying.

118  Within a minute, the doors opened.

119  Inside he found a big white swan and a dirty man from the mine standing solemnly together inside a veil of fog.

* * *

120  Three sets of blinks: logger blink, miner blink, swan blink.

121  Clouds don't blink.

122  "Oh it's you," said the miner at last. "We met in the mine. I was wondering when I'd bump into you up here."

123  The logger nodded. He was staring at the miner who he didn't recognize— the man's face was radiant, trumpets and playing sad marches beneath his skin. He had not seen a single man who looked like that in the mine, and he would've remembered.

124  "I'm looking for my axe," he said. "Seen any doves around here?"

125  The miner didn't respond. Next to him, the swan was trying to pull part of the thinning bluish fog onto its back.

126  "Come on, honey," he said. "Come on."

127  The miner tried to pick up the fog and put it on the swan's back but his hands went straight through, useless. He turned back to the logger.

128  "This elevator appears to be broken," he said. "Are you a repairman?"

129  "No," said the logger.

130  "Can you be a repairman?"

131  "No," said the logger. "All I do is chop things down. I'm the exact opposite of a repairman."

132  "Well, we need to get this cloud back to the sky," said the swan. "It's of **dire** importance. It's too thin to sit on my back anymore so I can't fly it up."

133  "Come on my back," the swan said again, to the fog. "Come on, baby."

134  "That's no cloud," said the logger, and the swan hung his neck in shame.

135  The miner glared. "Can't you see," he said, "that's not very helpful."

NOTES

136   The logger stepped into the elevator. "You sure you haven't seen any doves?" he asked again.

137   The swan began whispering to the walls of the elevator in bird language, the words mysteriously lengthened and choppy at the same time, and the elevator seemed to creak and listen, but its doors did not shut and nothing moved upward. The cloud was so thin now it filled the whole elevator, filling the air with a blue-whiteness that made it hard to see, like living in the interior of a pearl. Only the swan's black beaded eyes shone through, wet and glassy and wretched with guilt.

138   The three of them stood there, waiting for something to happen. The logger kept flexing his hands. The miner's eyes were closed, remembering.

139   The cloud's vagueness began moving into the lobby itself now.

140   "Shut the lobby doors," ordered the swan, "Hurry! We can't let it get any thinner than the size of the lobby."

141   The miner ran to the glass doors on either end and shut both firmly. Off cue, the bark elevator opened and released a few logs on the ground, like an awkward phrase spoken out of turn at a party by a guest no one is listening to.

142   "I need my axe!" the logger cried out. The agitation was growing in his palms.

143   The swan was weeping openly now, his child the size of the whole lobby.

144   The miner picked up a log and leaned his nose into the wood, breathing in, the smell elemental. "Hey," he said to the logger. "Those doves did come by," he said. "They had an axe, a watch, some gold nuggets, I think a tiny mink coat. Anyway, they flew by, but when they saw the elevator was broken, they left to go somewhere else."

145   The logger's jaw dropped. "You saw the doves?" he said.

146   "This was hours ago," said the miner. "They're long gone."

147   "They had my axe?" said the logger.

148   "And some fur. And gold," said the miner. "And a watch. They're set for a while, those doves."

149   The logger's heart sank like a rock. The swan stepped out of the elevator, neck low and broken as an old daisy stem, and now that all three were out of

Please note that excerpts and passages in the StudySync® library and this workbook are intended as touchstones to generate interest in an author's work. The excerpts and passages do not substitute for the reading of entire texts, and StudySync® strongly recommends that students seek out and purchase the whole literary or informational work in order to experience it as the author intended. Links to online resellers are available in our digital library. In addition, complete works may be ordered through an authorized reseller by filling out and returning to StudySync® the order form enclosed in this workbook.

Reading & Writing
Companion

83

it, standing in the lobby, covered in mist and fog, the feather elevator doors closed with a whir, and it began its rise up.

150  "No! Wait!" cried the swan, but it was too late. The feather elevator was already ascending, the box replaced by a pole in their line of vision.

\* \* \*

151  The elevator stayed up for ten hours and the swan would not let the miner or the logger leave the lobby through the side doors because he didn't want his cloud child to dissipate further.

152  "We're stuck here forever," said the swan. "I'm sorry to have to tell you both that, but if you try to leave, I will peck out your eyes."

153  The logger stared at the pole of the feather elevator.

154  The miner wanted to go back to the sky.

155  The logger suggested he take the other elevators out, but the miner didn't want to.

156  "I'm waiting for that," he said, pointing up.

157  The logger didn't know where to go. He could not go back down to the mine where they hated him or to the forest where he was a shame on his father's name. So he sat down. The swan was smoothing down his feathers, one at a time. The fog was still thick enough to make the logger sleepy, so he curled up on the hard tile and closed his eyes.

\* \* \*

158  Come morning, outside the lobby, the bluebird tapped her beak against the glass.

159  "Our egg opened!" she cried out.

160  The swan woke up, chilled from the fog, and pressed his beak against the glass, where it made a triangular smear mark.

161  His eyes were bright and shining, desperate.

162  "Is it alive?" he asked.

163  She nodded, vigorously.

164 "Very," she said through the glass. "It's a lake. A big deep blue one. I floated around on it all evening waiting for you. You should've seen it pour straight out of the shell, for minutes and minutes and minutes, so much water in that one little shell, and then it knew just what to do, how to settle itself."

165 She glimpsed past her husband's great wings.

166 "What are you doing holding our firstborn hostage like that?" she asked.

167 "We had a lake?" he said.

168 She laughed. Her wing feathers were damp. "Let the poor cloud out!" she said. "Poor thing has been cooped up all night! How I love a good cool fog."

169 She hopped over to the lobby door and with some difficulty opened it herself. Within seconds, the fog swooshed out into the air, wrapping around the trunks of trees like cotton, exiting grandly.

170 The swan felt his heart contract then expand, palpitate then release, and with his head and neck a question mark, he left the sleeping miner and the sleeping logger and went to where the nest was. Sure enough, right by the bundle of indented twigs, there was now a small lake with a pretty shore and all sorts of bugs treading the surface. A graceful sapling grew by the side. There was a hint of dampness in the air. The swan stood close to his wife, white feathers melding with her blue ones into a makeshift sky of their own.

171 "Welcome to our family," the swan said meekly. Water lapped over his feet.

* * *

172 After an hour, the logger and miner woke up in the lobby, doors wide open, swan gone, the sunlight bright and shining and hot, the fog cleared. The miner squinted. The feather elevator was back down, its door open also. He went right inside. The doors began closing but he put his foot in the crucial area that stops the close of every elevator and called to the just-waking logger to join him.

173 The logger shook his head.

174 The miner just smiled. "You have something better to do?" he asked.

175 So the logger, bleary from a night of bad dreams, stepped forward, and the two men stood in the elevator. To the miner's purest joy, the doors closed and the elevator rose high, higher, highest, up those forty-five stories.

176 The logger wiped his eyes clean of sleep and said, "I don't know what—"

NOTES

177    And the miner said: "This."

178    As if they had heard, the feather elevator doors opened. It was a bright warm spring morning and far below they could see the new sparkling lake that the white swan and blue bluebird swam upon. The forest spread out in a green blanket. The castle glittered in the distance like a wedding cake.

179    "Everything I need," said the miner, sweeping his hand out.

180    The logger's heart was failing. He took a deep breath and looked down. The miner was saying something about the approaching rise of the sun. The logger didn't listen and flung himself out the door of the elevator into the air.

* * *

181    The fall was fast and cold, with blur and clarity both, everything a sheet downward while he saw in detail the flying birds, then the treetops, then the red roofs of houses, then doors, then roots, and he fell like a stone and was certain to die if something of a wind hadn't held and pushed him enough to the right, landing him in the middle of the small newborn lake that was occupied by one swan, one bluebird, and a thousand spinning insects.

182    He fell and struck through, and the water was like glass, but still it broke beneath him and so then he did not have to break.

* * *

183    The miner watched with horror up in his elevator, side by side, gone in a slim fall. He saw the water crash up around the logger's weight, then the swan and bluebird pull the logger from the water, cover him with leaves, and put cloaks of feathers over his brittle body.

184    The bluebird brought him leaf after leaf until he was blanketed. The lake resettled agreeably and returned to mirror. The swan smoothed the logger's forehead, which was heavy with pain, and found the logger to be so agitated that he went to see his old friend the queen. The queen was terribly glad to see her old friend the swan, and they sat in the palace garden while ladybugs flew off the bushes and landed on their faces and backs.

185    "He has nothing to do," said the swan, eating a ladybug. "He feels he has no purpose."

186    The queen took a sip of her turtle tea. "Perhaps," she said, "I can find a job for him," she said. "I'll look into it. And how is your first-born?"

187    The swan hung his head. "I may have chased him off for good," he said.

Copyright © BookheadEd Learning, LLC

188   The queen patted the swan's noble skull under those smooth white feathers. She offered her friend a mug of hedge tea. The swan stuck his black beak inside the narrow mouth of the porcelain and drank down the strange dark liquid herbs.

\* \* \*

189   The bluebird called the logger her third child, delivered from the air, from that feather egg cracking open in the sky. "I always wanted three," she told him, nodding.

190   "I want my axe," the logger said, curled up on the ground.

191   The bluebird blinked and brushed his cheek gently with the tip of her wing.

\* \* \*

192   There was now a search party for the missing miner. A couple of men with bags under their eyes and a pasty look were snooping around the lobby looking for him. "He's up there," said the swan, on the way back from his visit with the queen. He pointed with his wing. "Where?" they said, and the swan pointed again, to the small gray box in the sky that was the feather elevator. "Well, we need him downstairs," shouted the men. "No one's as good a worker as he is!"

193   "I won't come down!" yelled the miner, from forty-five stories up. "I will never go back in that mine!"

194   "It's your JOB," called the miners, "we need you! Productivity has plummeted."

195   "Never!" shouted the miner from forty-five stories up. The elevator stood firm in its post above the trees.

196   "It's an order," mumbled the miners.

197   Neither one of them was really breathing in the air or noticing the trees, but one did have a shovel and began chopping at the pole that held up that feather elevator. The shovel was not a sharp blade but he kept hacking away because he was a miner, after all, and used to repetitive movement.

198   Ten minutes away, sitting on the edge of the lake, the sound of chipping metal pricked up the logger's ears. He stumbled to the lobby and found the two miners crouched at the feather elevator pole, chopping away.

199   "You can't do that," he murmured. "You have to leave him there. He's found his calling in the world: air. His calling is air."

200  His voice was meek and tentative, and his legs wobbly, still, from the fall. The other miners ignored him, as he stood there in the lobby, quivering, watching these two men as they chopped, with hideous form, he had to admit, making ineffective dents in the pole. And while he was standing there, right on time, the two other elevators opened and released their goods at the exact same moment. He himself had never seen that before.

201  The metal and timber collectors hadn't arrived yet, and there he was, standing among the two piles.

202  Metal and wood were two ingredients necessary to make the one thing he needed most in the world. He stooped down at the elevator doors, and slowly, with a heavy feeling in his chest, picked up four nuggets of gold and a nice hard oak log. He left the chipping miner jerks and ran with the gold and wood over to the workshop where loggers made their tools. There he spent the whole day, working as fast and neatly as he could, his hand muscles remembering the lessons he had learned as a young boy, fingers flying over the sanding machine, the metal cutter, the blowtorch, the saw, making the best alloy of gold and steel, the best handle of oak and elm, sweating until he'd built a brand new axe, glowing with a golden blade, the handle as smooth as a pebble on the beach. The sun was about to set, and he hoisted it over his shoulder and marched back to the men chopping at the feather elevator.

203  "Stop!" he said loudly.

204  By now, the miners had eaten away at about a fourth of the pole, with messy choppy bites from the shovel. It was starting to affect the balance and the pole swayed just the slightest bit in the breeze.

205  They eyed the glittering axe in the logger's hands. He looked exactly right holding it.

206  "Or what," they said nervously.

207  "Or I'll chop off your heads," said the logger.

208  And he meant it. He didn't really want to chop off any heads, or well, he kind of did, but he kind of didn't, and mostly he wanted to make sure that the adventurous miner would stay put in the sky for as long as he damn well pleased.

209  The other miners put their shovels down.

210  "But we need him in the mine," they whined.

211 "Too bad," said the logger, and the two men stood there for a moment, deciding, and then slunk back down with the gold elevator, shoulders low.

212 The logger was so excited to have an axe again, he went around town and chopped down a mess of stuff, including someone's birdhouse and another person's lamplight. The new blade was even better than his last, this one so sharp from the steel and also so beautiful in the various lights of day—honey gold at sunset, brassy gold at noon, lemon gold at dawn.

213 When he came home that evening, he found the miner shimmying down the elevator pole.

214 "I got hungry," the miner said, once on the ground, gingerly touching the raw insides of his arms.

215 "They want you back," said the logger.

216 The miner shook his head and walked over to the lake where he found the swan and bluebird tucked into each other, floating.

217 "I'm leaving," he said, bowing slightly. "I want to thank you all very much for your tremendous friendship and kindness."

218 The bluebird and the swan swam to the shore, and the miner walked over and gave each a hug: the sweet chirping bluebird, the warm soft feathers of the swan, the stalwart tall logger. Everyone's eyes misted for a minute. Then the miner took off down the lane, a lift in his step, whistling melodic melodies, humming in minor miner keys.

\* \* \*

219 Word got out about the man with the axe made of strong gold, and after a day or so, the king and queen asked the logger if he would please finish the job and chop down that feather elevator, as it had not come down since the other miners had bit at its core and was now a problem with air traffic control. Now that the miner was gone, the logger set to it, and his shoulders and wrists were in bliss, immediately. The act of chopping made him feel so right and the elevator creaked and he knew just the angle to make a quiet fall, a slow— Tim-ber!— over a period of minutes. He ate at that metal pole until it began to creak and sway and at last dipped down, elegant, lying on the ground like a felled column of smoke. Then he removed the feather box from its pole and brought it to the castle, a room of feathers to sit in for those who needed a little special peace and quiet. The queen liked to sit in the feather box very much, as it reminded him of the friend she missed, who smelled exactly like it.

Copyright © BookheadEd Learning, LLC

220    The other two elevators kept operating on schedule, with an empty space where the third had been. Some birds set up a nest in there.

221    The logger was appointed Earl of Down.

\* \* \*

222    In the evenings, after he'd done his duty chopping down items for the palace, the logger walked to the lake, swinging his golden axe over his shoulder, and spent time with the swan and the bluebird. A few weeks or so after the cutting down of the third elevator, the three friends sat around by the lakeshore, watching the spinning bugs make the smallest circles, missing the miner. It was almost twilight, and the air grew moist with night.

223    "I bet he went to the ocean," said the swan. "He said he wanted to see something big."

224    The logger nodded. He liked to think of that miner, walking and whistling and breathing the air. He took a leaf off the ground and began polishing the gold blade of his axe until it nearly bent under the warmth in his hands.

225    The swan smoothed the feathers in his wings.

226    The bluebird preened herself by the shores of the lake. "Oh look, look," she said, whispering into the water. "Isn't this lovely. Here's your brother now."

227    And from the west, like a long slow breath, the fog was rolling in.

Aimee Bender is the author of the story collections *The Girl in the Flammable Skirt* and *Willful Creatures* and the novels *An Invisible Sign of My Own* and *The Particular Sadness of Lemon Cake*.

the
third
elevator

# First Read

Read "The Third Elevator." After you read, complete the Think Questions below.

## ☁ THINK QUESTIONS

1. What is "troublesome" about the main logger in the story? Cite specific details to help explain why the logger is seen this way. What is the source of his "troublesome" nature?

2. How does the young miner react when the adventurous miner brings him to the world above ground? Cite evidence from the story illustrating how the young miner feels about the new things he is seeing and experiencing.

3. What is unique about the two eggs that the bluebird hatched? In two to three sentences, use the text to describe what was in the eggs. What might have caused the contents of these eggs to be so different from normal eggs?

4. The other loggers believe that the "troublesome" logger is being **melodramatic**. Based on his behavior, what do you think the word *melodramatic* means? Write your best definition of the word here and explain how you arrived at its meaning.

5. The word **claustrophobia** combines the Latin word *claustrum*, meaning "barrier," and the Greek word *phobos*, meaning "fear." Use this information to determine the meaning of *claustrophobia* in paragraphs 35 and 46. Write your best definition here and explain how you figured it out.

Please note that excerpts and passages in the StudySync® library and this workbook are intended as touchstones to generate interest in an author's work. The excerpts and passages do not substitute for the reading of entire texts, and StudySync® strongly recommends that students seek out and purchase the whole literary or informational work in order to experience it as the author intended. Links to online resellers are available in our digital library. In addition, complete works may be ordered through an authorized reseller by filling out and returning to StudySync® the order form enclosed in this workbook.

Reading & Writing Companion

91

# Skill:
# Character

Use the Checklist to analyze Character in "The Third Elevator." Refer to the sample student annotations about Character in the text.

## ••• CHECKLIST FOR CHARACTER

In order to determine how particular elements of a story or drama interact, note the following:

- ✓ the characters in the story, including the protagonist and antagonist

- ✓ the settings and how they shape the characters or plot

- ✓ plot events and how they affect the characters

- ✓ key events or a series of episodes in the plot, especially events that cause characters to react, respond, or change in some way

- ✓ characters' responses as the plot reaches a climax and moves toward a resolution of the problem facing the protagonist

- ✓ the resolution of the conflict in the plot and the ways that resolution affects each character

To analyze how particular elements of a story or drama interact, consider the following questions:

- ✓ How do the characters' responses change or develop from the beginning to the end of the story?

- ✓ How does the setting shape the characters and plot in the story?

- ✓ How do the events in the plot affect the characters? How do characters develop as a result of the conflict, climax, and resolution?

- ✓ Do the characters' problems reach a resolution? How?

- ✓ How does the resolution affect the characters?

# Skill:
# Character

Reread paragraphs 45–47 of "The Third Elevator." Then, using the Checklist on the previous page, answer the multiple-choice questions below.

## 🔄 YOUR TURN

1. Based on the description of the miner in paragraph 45, the reader can conclude that —

   ○ A. the miner is lazy and wants to ride in the elevator.
   ○ B. the miner is curious to see what is above ground.
   ○ C. the miner is tired of getting passed over for promotions.
   ○ D. the miner is very satisfied with his job as a miner.

2. This question has two parts. First, answer Part A. Then, answer Part B.

   **Part A:** What do the miner's thoughts and actions in paragraph 46 reveal about him?

   ○ A. He is confident about taking the gold elevator.
   ○ B. He is frustrated with the other miners on his team.
   ○ C. He is anxious to breathe fresh air again.
   ○ D. He is confused about the logger's whereabouts.

   **Part B:** Which of the following details best supports your response to Part A?

   ○ A. "One of the miners, who regularly filled up the gold elevator and was considered one of the best workers, had watched the logger go up the elevator with curiosity and envy."
   ○ B. "He hadn't known a person could take that trip."
   ○ C. "So, a few hours after the logger had left, the miner told his workmates that he was going to follow that logger and get in the elevator when half the load was full because he had to see the top of the earth again or he was going to die of claustrophobia of the lungs."
   ○ D. "The miners were a supportive team, because they had to be or they'd all be dead, and so they let him hop inside the gold elevator right before it went up, watching the doors close over his nervous face, cheeks reflecting the piles of metal as if he'd been working for years in sunshine."

# Close Read

Reread "The Third Elevator." As you reread, complete the Skills Focus questions below. Then use your answers and annotations from the questions to help you complete the Write activity.

## ◎ SKILLS FOCUS

1. Identify figurative language that helps develop the swan's personality in the beginning of "The Third Elevator." Explain how that language helps you to understand his behavior with his first child later in the story.

2. Recall that in an omniscient point of view, the narrator reveals thoughts and feelings. In a limited point point of view, a narrator does not refer to thoughts and feelings but describes only what can be heard or seen. Identify evidence of the point of view used to describe the main logger, and explain how this point of view develops the reader's understanding of the story.

3. Identify evidence of the bluebird's behavior in the story, and explain how it influences the other characters.

4. The miner and logger are both looking for a place where they belong. Identify examples of the theme of belonging in the text, and explain what the author has to say about this theme.

5. Myths and folktales often include talking animals that help to express the author's ideas. Identify examples of this element in the story, and explain why this element is still relevant to help express an important idea in the text.

## ✏ WRITE

LITERARY ANALYSIS: Identify a theme or lesson in this text about family, friendship, or a sense of belonging. How do characters' actions and the author's use of fantasy develop this important idea about real life? Remember to use evidence from the text to support and explain your response.

# Perseus

POETRY
Robert Hayden
1966

## Introduction

Widely acclaimed for his poetry about the black historical experience, Robert Hayden (1913–1980) was the first African American to serve as Consultant in Poetry to the Library of Congress. Here, Hayden offers a new perspective on the Greek mythical hero Perseus. Gazing down on the severed head of Medusa, the snake-haired Gorgon, Perseus has a moment of self-reflection and acknowledges his powerful and dangerous "thirst ... to destroy."

# "I struck. The shield flashed bare."

**Skill:**
Connotation
and Denotation

*The description refers
to the snakes on
Medusa's head. The
word* serpents *means
"snakes," which has a
neutral connotation.*
Serpents, *however, has
strong negative
connotations—it is
associated with
monsters, and evil.*

1   Her sleeping head with its great **gelid** mass
2   of serpents **torpidly** astir[1]
3   burned into the mirroring shield—
4   a **scathing** image **dire**
5   as hated truth the mind accepts at last
6   and **festers** on.
7   I struck. The shield flashed bare.

8   Yet even as I lifted up the head
9   and started from that place
10  of gazing silences and terrored stone,
11  I thirsted to destroy.
12  None could have passed me then—
13  no garland-bearing girl, no priest
14  or staring boy—and lived.

"Perseus." Copyright ©1966 by Robert Hayden, from COLLECTED POEMS
OF ROBERT HAYDEN by Robert Hayden, edited by Frederick Glaysher.
Copyright ©1985 by Emma Hayden. Used by permission of Liveright
Publishing Corporation.

---

1. **astir** moving about, usually excitedly; active

# First Read

Read "Perseus." After you read, complete the Think Questions below.

## ☁ THINK QUESTIONS

1. What does line 10 tell you about the setting of Medusa's resting place? Explain, using evidence from the text to support your answer.

2. How is Perseus able to behead the snake-haired Medusa without turning to "terrored stone"? Cite textual evidence to support your answer.

3. After Perseus kills Medusa, what "hated truth" does he acknowledge about himself? Cite textual evidence to support your answer.

4. Use context clues to determine the meaning of **gelid** as it is used in line 1 of "Perseus." Write your definition here, and identify clues that helped you figure out the meaning. Then check the meaning in a dictionary.

5. Find the word **torpidly** in line 2 of "Perseus." Use context clues in the surrounding lines, as well as the stanza in which the word appears, to determine the word's meaning. Write your definition here and identify clues that helped you figure out its meaning.

Please note that excerpts and passages in the StudySync® library and this workbook are intended as touchstones to generate interest in an author's work. The excerpts and passages do not substitute for the reading of entire texts, and StudySync® strongly recommends that students seek out and purchase the whole literary or informational work in order to experience it as the author intended. Links to online resellers are available in our digital library. In addition, complete works may be ordered through an authorized reseller by filling out and returning to StudySync® the order form enclosed in this workbook.

Reading & Writing Companion    97

# Skill:
# Connotation and Denotation

Use the Checklist to analyze Connotation and Denotation in "Perseus." Refer to the sample student annotations about Connotation and Denotation in the text.

## ••• CHECKLIST FOR CONNOTATION AND DENOTATION

In order to identify the connotative meanings of words and phrases, use the following steps:

✓ first, note unfamiliar words and phrases; key words used to describe important characters, events, and ideas; or words that inspire an emotional reaction

✓ next, determine and note the denotative meaning of words by consulting reference materials such as a dictionary, glossary, or thesaurus

To better understand the meaning of words and phrases as they are used in a text, including connotative meanings, use the following questions:

✓ What is the genre or subject of the text? How does that affect the possible meaning of a word or phrase?

✓ Does the word create a positive, negative, or neutral emotion?

✓ What synonyms or alternative phrasing help you describe the connotative meaning of the word?

To determine the meaning of words and phrases as they are used in a text, including connotative meanings, use the following questions:

✓ What is the meaning of the word or phrase? What is the connotation as well as the denotation?

✓ If I substitute a synonym based on denotation, is the meaning the same? How does it change the meaning of the text?

# Skill:
# Connotation and Denotation

Reread the second stanza (lines 8–14) of "Perseus." Then, using the Checklist on the previous page, answer the multiple-choice questions below.

## ↻ YOUR TURN

1. This question has two parts. First, answer Part A. Then, answer Part B.

   **Part A:** Which answer best describes the connotation of the word *thirsted*?

   ○ A. hate with the whole heart          ○ C. want badly or crave
   ○ B. be trembling with fear             ○ D. want to drink

   **Part B:** Which textual evidence best supports your answer to Part A?

   ○ A. None could have passed me then . . . and lived.
   ○ B. no garland-bearing girl, no priest / or staring boy
   ○ C. from that place / of gazing silences and terrored stone
   ○ D. Yet even as I lifted up the head / and started from that place

2. This question has two parts. First, answer Part A. Then, answer Part B.

   **Part A:** In line 13 of "Perseus," how does the phrase "garland-bearing girl" help the reader to understand Perseus's mood?

   ○ A. A "garland-bearing girl" connotes that Perseus would harm someone who is playful.
   ○ B. A "garland-bearing girl" connotes that Perseus would harm someone who is quiet.
   ○ C. A "garland-bearing girl" connotes that Perseus would harm someone who is peaceful and nonthreatening.
   ○ D. A "garland-bearing girl" connotes that Perseus hates flowers.

   **Part B:** Which lines from the poem best support your answer to Part A?

   ○ A. lines 4 and 5          ○ C. lines 1 and 2
   ○ B. lines 6 and 7          ○ D. lines 1–3

Copyright © BookheadEd Learning, LLC

# Close Read

Reread "Perseus." As you reread, complete the Skills Focus questions below. Then use your answers and annotations from the questions to help you complete the Write activity.

## ◎ SKILLS FOCUS

1. Use context clues to define the word *mass* as it is used in line 1 of the poem. Analyze why the poet uses this word rather than a synonym. What does this word's connotation suggest about Medusa?

2. What do you notice about the structure of the sentences that make up the first stanza? Explain how this structure impacts the tone of the stanza.

3. Explain the poet's use of the phrase "gazing silences" in line 10. Cite textual evidence by highlighting clues that explain its meaning, and make annotations to explore the connotations of the words.

4. How do the examples Perseus provides in lines 13 and 14 impact the meaning of what he is telling his audience at the end of the poem? How do they fit in with the poem's tone? Highlight and explain specific examples of words and phrases to support your thinking.

5. How are Perseus's experiences relevant to readers today? What lessons can be learned from Perseus's actions? How do they inform us? Support your ideas with textual evidence.

## ✎ WRITE

LITERARY ANALYSIS: "Perseus" shares with readers the inner struggle of a hero who finds that he is more like his enemy than he realized. How does the author's word choice show Perseus's inner conflict and the poem's meaning? How does the word choice impact the poem's tone? Write a short response answering these questions. Support your writing with specific examples of connotations of words and phrases from the text.

Extended
Writing
Project and
Grammar

EXTENDED
WRITING
PROJECT
RESEARCH WRITING

# Research Writing Process: Plan

| PLAN | DRAFT | REVISE | EDIT AND PUBLISH |
|---|---|---|---|

Many of the fables, myths, and folktales that you have read include references to people, places, things, and events from different time periods and cultures. *Aesop's Fables* gives readers insight into ancient values. "The Classical Roots of 'The Hunger Games'" explains how *The Hunger Games* draws inspiration from female Amazon warriors, ancient gladiators, and the Latin language. A reader's curiosity could pull him or her into a variety of topics after reading such rich texts.

## WRITING PROMPT

**Consider the texts that you've read in this unit. What stories or ideas stood out to you? What topic would you like to know more about?**

Identify a research topic and write a report about that topic using an informational text structure. In the process, you will learn how to select a research question, develop a research plan, gather and evaluate source materials, and synthesize and present your research findings. Regardless of which topic you choose, be sure your research paper includes the following:

- an introduction to the research question
- a clear thesis statement that informs the reader
- supporting details from credible sources
- a clear informational text structure
- a conclusion that wraps up your ideas
- a works cited page

### Writing to Sources

As you gather ideas and information from the texts in the unit, be sure to:

- use evidence from multiple sources
- avoid overly relying on one source

**Introduction to Research Writing**

Research writing examines a topic and conveys ideas by citing and analyzing information from credible sources. Good research papers use textual evidence, including facts, statistics, examples, and details from reliable sources, to supply information about a topic and to support the analysis of complex ideas. They also can include relevant print and graphic features as well as multimedia. Research helps writers not only to discover and confirm facts, but also to draw new conclusions about a topic. The characteristics of research writing include:

- an introduction that presents information on your topic with a clear thesis statement
- relevant facts, supporting details, and quotations from credible sources
- analysis of the details to explain how they support the thesis statement
- a clear and logical informational text structure
- a formal style
- a conclusion that wraps up your ideas
- a works cited page

As you continue with this Extended Writing Project, you'll receive more instruction and practice in crafting each of the characteristics of research writing to create your own research paper.

Before you get started on your own research paper, read this research paper that one student, Nicole, wrote in response to the writing prompt. As you read the Model, highlight and annotate the features of research writing that Nicole included in her research paper.

## ☰ STUDENT MODEL

### The Storyteller's Legacy

1   Henry Louis Gates, Jr., co-editor of the new anthology *The Annotated African American Folktales*, dedicates the volume to his three-year-old granddaughter. Gates hopes that the collection will help future generations feel as if the stories are as much theirs as they once were his (Siegel). Gates and his co-editor, Maria Tatar, are two links in a very long chain of storytellers who have worked to keep the oral tradition of storytelling alive. These two are not alone. Why is the oral tradition so important to African American culture? Oral tradition is extremely important in African American culture due to its history of preserving culture and legacy in Africa, in early America, and in modern times.

### Storytelling Roots in Africa

2   Storytelling began as a way of preserving culture during a time before writing was common. In early Africa, few languages were written; literature was handed down orally. Griots, or storytellers, collected songs and stories as a way of protecting and sharing cultural values and customs. Without written records, these griots had to hold a culture's important information within their brains. Franklin and Moss note, "They kept in their memories the history, law, and traditions of their people and were themselves living dictionaries" (28). As such, storytellers were valuable and honored members of the community.

3   The oral tradition affected every part of Africans' lives. For these early societies, speech was more than a means of communication. It was power. Janice D. Hamlet explains, "The Africans believed in Nommo, which means the generative power of the spoken word. Nommo was believed necessary to actualize life and give man mastery over things" (27). Speaking allowed these Africans to feel in control over their world. This part of the oral tradition would become especially valuable in the years to come, as many Africans were taken against their will and forced into slavery.

**Oral Tradition in Early America**

4   When the enslaved Africans were brought to America, they lost almost everything. They lost their homes, their friends and families, and, most importantly, their freedom. Yet, there was one thing they were able to bring with them: their oral traditions. Folktales were a way to bond and to preserve African culture in a new and hostile environment: "Told at night, for entertainment as well as instruction, in the traditional African style in which the entire community might be involved in the telling, these stories as performances provided entertainment by which the community could celebrate its identity as a group simply by singing, dancing, and most important, laughing together" (Abrahams 18).

5    Storytelling was an escape from the struggles of their daily lives. Its connection to community values brought comfort. Furthermore, storytelling could provide support through hidden messages. Enslaved people could not express themselves openly; instead, they put their fears, hopes, and support for one another within stories. Such stories often featured animals instead of people. When these stories were overheard, slaveholders did not know what the enslaved people were really talking about. In this way, enslaved people could regain their voices as well as a sense of power (Abrahams 9). The oral tradition had an important practical function, too. An observer might have thought enslaved people were singing "Follow the Drinking Gourd" or "Swing Low, Sweet Chariot" to pass the time, but the lyrics actually concealed coded messages that showed the route to freedom via the Underground Railroad (Hudson 206–207). More than 150 years after the abolition of slavery in the United States, these songs remain an important part of African American culture.

**The Oral Tradition Continues Today**

6    Today, African American cultural values and customs are shared in many different ways; nevertheless, the lasting effect of the oral tradition is clear. Nommo still plays an active role in African American culture, both in the call-and-response style of African American church services and in hip-hop culture (Hamlet 28). A rap song may seem very different from a traditional folktale, but both share the same heritage.

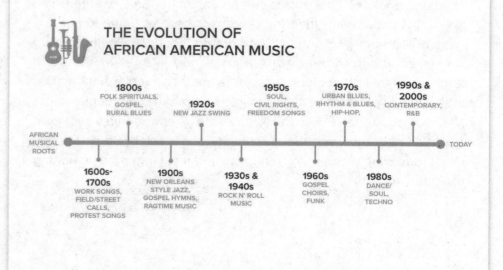

THE EVOLUTION OF
AFRICAN AMERICAN MUSIC

1800s
FOLK SPIRITUALS,
GOSPEL,
RURAL BLUES

1920s
NEW JAZZ SWING

1950s
SOUL,
CIVIL RIGHTS,
FREEDOM SONGS

1970s
URBAN BLUES,
RHYTHM & BLUES,
HIP-HOP,

1990s &
2000s
CONTEMPORARY,
R&B

AFRICAN
MUSICAL
ROOTS

TODAY

1600s-
1700s
WORK SONGS,
FIELD/STREET
CALLS,
PROTEST SONGS

1900s
NEW ORLEANS
STYLE JAZZ,
GOSPEL HYMNS,
RAGTIME MUSIC

1930s &
1940s
ROCK N' ROLL
MUSIC

1960s
GOSPEL
CHOIRS,
FUNK

1980s
DANCE/
SOUL,
TECHNO

7  Storytelling helps us to better understand our past, our present, and our place in the world. Jeff Wallenfeldt says, "It is inevitable, if not essential, that performers take images from the present and wed them to the past, and in that way the past regularly shapes any audience's experience of the present. Storytellers reveal connections between humans—within the world, within a society, within a tribe, within a family" (77). Stories affect us deeply; they form links across generations and across cultures. Every time a story is told, it becomes part of the listener. When enough people hear and share the tale, it becomes a part of our experience. Maybe closeness, not entertainment, is the goal of storytelling: "Perhaps the real reason that we tell stories again and again—and endlessly praise our greatest storytellers—is because humans want to be a part of a shared history" (Delistraty). Differences still separate groups of people in today's society; telling stories helps us focus on what we have in common.

8  In early Africa, griots told stories to help their community remember where they came from. Over hundreds of years, not much has changed. Authors and storytellers as well as editors like Gates and Tatar have retold traditional stories to help today's audiences understand our shared past and to help shape our future. At bedtime, parents can often be found telling their children old stories, not new inventions, because those are the stories their parents once told them. A story may change a bit each time it's told; however, the way stories help us connect with each other remains the same.

Please note that excerpts and passages in the StudySync® library and this workbook are intended as touchstones to generate interest in an author's work. The excerpts and passages do not substitute for the reading of entire texts, and StudySync® strongly recommends that students seek out and purchase the whole literary or informational work in order to experience it as the author intended. Links to online resellers are available in our digital library. In addition, complete works may be ordered through an authorized reseller by filling out and returning to StudySync® the order form enclosed in this workbook.

Reading & Writing Companion    107

NOTES

## Works Cited

Abrahams, Roger, D. *Afro-American Folktales: Stories from Black Traditions in the New World*. Pantheon, 1995.

Delistraty, Cody C. "The Psychological Comforts of Storytelling." *The Atlantic*, 2 Nov. 2014, www.theatlantic.com/health/archive/2014/11/the-psychological-comforts-of-storytelling/381964/.

Franklin, John Hope, and Alfred A. Moss, Jr. *From Slavery to Freedom: A History of African Americans*. Knopf, 2000.

Hamlet, Janice D. "Word! The African American Oral Tradition and Its Rhetorical Impact on American Popular Culture." *Black History Bulletin*, vol. 74, no. 1, 2011, pp. 27–29.

Hudson, J. Blaine. *Encyclopedia of the Underground Railroad*. McFarland, 2006.

Siegel, Robert. "'Annotated African American Folktales' Reclaims Stories Passed Down from Slavery." *All Things Considered*, National Public Radio, 10 Nov. 2017, www.npr.org/2017/11/10/563110377/annotated-african-american-folktales-reclaims-stories-passed-down-from-slavery.

Wallenfeldt, Jeff. *Africa to America: From the Middle Passage Through the 1930s*. Rosen, 2010.

# ✎ WRITE

Writers often take notes about ideas before they sit down to write. Think about what you've learned so far about organizing research writing to help you begin prewriting.

- What topic from the unit do you find most interesting? What will you research?

- What do you already know about this topic? What else do you want to learn about the topic?

- Who is your audience and what do you want to inform them about?

- How can you use a question or questions to focus your research?

**Response Instructions**

Use the questions in the bulleted list to write a one-paragraph research summary. Your summary should describe the topic that you plan to research and discuss what you hope to learn about this topic. Make sure to include at least one question that will guide and focus your research as you write this informative research paper.

Don't worry about including all of the details now; focus only on the most essential and important elements. You will refer back to this short summary as you continue through the steps of the writing process.

# Skill:
# Planning Research

## ••• CHECKLIST FOR PLANNING RESEARCH

In order to develop a short research project to answer a question drawing on several sources, do the following:

- Make a list of research tasks.

  > If it is not assigned to you, decide on a major research question.

  > Develop a research plan, a series of steps you can follow to find information to answer your question.

- Search for information.

  > Look for information on your topic, drawing on several sources both online and in books and other reference material.

  > If you don't find the information that you need to answer your major research question, you may need to modify it.

  > Generate additional related, focused questions for further research and investigation.

  > Refocus and revise your research plan as needed.

To develop a short research project to answer a question drawing on several sources, consider the following questions:

- How does the source address ideas, concepts, or other areas related to my research?

- Is my research question too broad or too focused?

- Do I need to change or reconsider my major research question?

- Does information in one source contradict or disprove information in another source? How might I resolve these differences?

##  YOUR TURN

Read the research questions below. Then, complete the chart by placing each question in the correct category.

| | Research Questions |
|---|---|
| **A** | What were ancient Romans like? |
| **B** | How did smugglers help refugees get across the Afghanistan–Pakistan border in the 1980s? |
| **C** | Why do refugees have to flee their home countries? |
| **D** | Why did people admire warriors in ancient Rome? |
| **E** | What kinds of Cinderella stories are told throughout the world? |
| **F** | What issues were causing Afghans to flee their homes and go to Pakistan? |
| **G** | Why are the morals in "The Invisible One" and "Adelita" still important today? |
| **H** | What values were important to ancient Romans? |
| **I** | Did Thailand's Cinderella story, "Kao and the Golden Fish," change how sisters treated each other in the 1990s? |

| Too Narrow | Appropriate | Too Broad |
|---|---|---|
| | | |
| | | |
| | | |

Please note that excerpts and passages in the StudySync® library and this workbook are intended as touchstones to generate interest in an author's work. The excerpts and passages do not substitute for the reading of entire texts, and StudySync® strongly recommends that students seek out and purchase the whole literary or informational work in order to experience it as the author intended. Links to online resellers are available in our digital library. In addition, complete works may be ordered through an authorized reseller by filling out and returning to StudySync® the order form enclosed in this workbook.

Reading & Writing Companion

111

**YOUR TURN**

Complete the chart below by brainstorming a list of possible research questions. After you have at least four questions, reread and evaluate each question to determine whether it is too narrow, too broad, or just right. Then build your research plan.

| Outline | Research Plan |
| --- | --- |
| Possible Research Questions: | |
| Selected Research Question: | |
| Step 1: | |
| Step 2: | |
| Step 3: | |

# Skill:
# Evaluating Sources

## ••• CHECKLIST FOR EVALUATING SOURCES

First, reread the sources you gathered and identify the following:

- what kind of source it is, including video, audio, or text, and where the source comes from
- where information seems inaccurate, biased, or outdated
- where information seems irrelevant or incomplete

In order to use advanced searches to gather relevant, credible, and accurate print and digital sources, use the following questions as a guide:

- Is the material up-to-date or based on the most current information?
- Is the material published by a well-established, trustworthy source or expert author?
- Is the material factual, and can it be verified by another source?
- Are there specific terms or phrases in my research question that I can use to adjust my search?
- Can I use "and," "or," or "not" to expand or limit my search?
- Can I use quotation marks to search for exact phrases?

Please note that excerpts and passages in the StudySync® library and this workbook are intended as touchstones to generate interest in an author's work. The excerpts and passages do not substitute for the reading of entire texts, and StudySync® strongly recommends that students seek out and purchase the whole literary or informational work in order to experience it as the author intended. Links to online resellers are available in our digital library. In addition, complete works may be ordered through an authorized reseller by filling out and returning to StudySync® the order form enclosed in this workbook.

Reading & Writing
Companion

113

YOUR TURN

Read the factors below. Then, complete the chart by placing them into two categories: those that show a source is credible and reliable and those that do not.

| Factors | |
|---|---|
| A | The article is published on a personal blog of a well-known political satirist. |
| B | The author has a Ph.D. and works for a university. |
| C | The article is over 15 years old. |
| D | The article was just published within the last year using the most recent studies on the topic. |
| E | The text uses clear facts and strong logic. |
| F | The author has no last name. |

| Credible and Reliable | Not Credible and Reliable |
|---|---|
| | |
| | |
| | |

YOUR TURN

Complete the chart below by filling in the title and author of a source and answering the questions about it.

| Questions | Answers |
|---|---|
| **Source Title and Author:** | |
| **Reliable:** Is the source material up-to-date or based on the most current information? | |
| **Credible:** Is the material published by a well-established source or expert author? | |
| **Accurate:** Is the material factual, and can it be verified by another source? | |
| Should I use this source in my paper? | |

Please note that excerpts and passages in the StudySync® library and this workbook are intended as touchstones to generate interest in an author's work. The excerpts and passages do not substitute for the reading of entire texts, and StudySync® strongly recommends that students seek out and purchase the whole literary or informational work in order to experience it as the author intended. Links to online resellers are available in our digital library. In addition, complete works may be ordered through an authorized reseller by filling out and returning to StudySync® the order form enclosed in this workbook.

Reading & Writing Companion 115

# Skill:
# Research and Notetaking

## ••• CHECKLIST FOR RESEARCH AND NOTETAKING

In order to conduct short research projects, drawing on several sources and generating additional related, focused questions for further research and investigation, note the following:

- Think of a question you would like to have answered.

- Look up your topic in an encyclopedia to find general information.

- Find specific, up-to-date information in books and periodicals, on the Internet, and if appropriate, from interviews with experts.

- Use the library's computerized catalog to locate books on your topic, and if you need help finding or using any of these resources, ask a librarian.

- Make sure that each source you use is closely related to your topic.

- Based on your research, create additional focused questions to help you investigate your topic further.

To conduct short research projects, drawing on several sources and generating additional related, focused questions for further research and investigation, consider the following questions:

- Is the information relevant and related to my topic?

- Where could I look to find additional information?

- Is the information I have found current and up-to-date?

- What additional, focused questions could I generate to help me investigate my topic further?

## ⟳ YOUR TURN

Read each bullet point from Nicole's note cards below. Then, complete the chart by placing them into two categories: those that support the oral tradition during slavery and those that support storytelling today.

| | Bullet Points |
|---|---|
| **A** | Source 4: Storytelling helps us better understand our past, our present, and our place in the world (77). |
| **B** | *Additional Question*: How do African American musicians and artists today use storytelling in their songs or raps? |
| **C** | Source 3: Folktales were a way to preserve culture. The only belongings that enslaved Africans could bring were their storytelling traditions (4). |
| **D** | Source 5: Songs like "Follow the Drinking Gourd" and "Swing Low, Sweet Chariot" contained secret messages to help enslaved people escape (206–207). |
| **E** | Source 6: Gates says that storytelling is "like links in a chain," and he wants to make sure the chain continues (Siegel). |
| **F** | *Additional Question*: When and where did enslaved Africans tell folktales and sing songs? |

| The Oral Tradition During Slavery | Storytelling Today |
|---|---|
| | |
| | |
| | |

## ✎ WRITE

Use the steps in the checklist section to identify and gather relevant information from a variety of sources. Write note cards for your sources as well as related questions for further research and investigation. When you have finished, write a brief reflection summarizing some relevant information you researched from at least two sources. End the reflection by writing one or two related questions you still have.

# Research Writing Process: Draft

| PLAN | DRAFT | REVISE | EDIT AND PUBLISH |

You have already made progress toward writing your informative research paper. Now it is time to draft your informative research paper.

## ✎ WRITE

Use your plan and other responses in your Binder to draft your research paper. You may also have new ideas as you begin drafting. Feel free to explore those new ideas as you have them. You can also ask yourself these questions to ensure that your writing is focused, is organized, and provides evidence and elaboration:

- Have I written a clear thesis statement?
- Am I using a logical informational text structure?
- Have I synthesized information from a variety of sources that will support my thesis statement?

Before you submit your draft, read it over carefully. You want to be sure that you've responded to all aspects of the prompt.

Here is Nicole's research paper draft. As you read, identify how Nicole used her research question to create a thesis statement and her main ideas and choose the specific facts, details, and examples she uses to develop her ideas.

## ☰ STUDENT MODEL: FIRST DRAFT

NOTES

### The Storyteller's Legacy

Henry Louis Gates, Jr., dedicates the book *The Annotated African American Folktales* to his three-year-old granddaughter. Gates hopes that the collection will help another generation feel as if the stories are as much theirs as they once were his (Siegel). Gates and his co-editor, Maria Tatar, are two people who have worked to keep the oral tradition of storytelling alive. These two are not alone. Why is the oral tradition so important to African American culture? Oral tradition is important in African American culture due to its history of preserving culture and legacy in Africa, early america, and today.

### Storytelling in Africa

~~Storytelling began as a way of preserving culture during a time before writing was common. In early Africa, few languages were written, literature was handed down orally. Griots collected songs and stories as a way of protecting and sharing cultural values and customs. Storytellers were valuable members of the community. The oral tradition effected every part of Africans' lives. Speech was more than a means of communication. It was power. Janice D. Hamlet explains, "The Africans believed in Nommo, which means the generative power of the spoken word. Nommo was believed necessary to actualize life and give man mastery over things" (74). Speaking allowed these Africans to feel in control over their world.~~

Storytelling began as a way of preserving culture during a time before writing was common. In early Africa, few languages were written; literature was handed down orally. Griots, or storytellers, collected songs and stories as a way of protecting and sharing cultural values and customs. Without written records, these griots had to hold a culture's important information within their brains. Franklin and Moss note, "They kept in their memories the history, law, and traditions of their people and were themselves living

Skill: Critiquing Research

Nicole used her new note cards to add another section to her informative research paper. By reviewing and critiquing her research, Nicole was able to gather more information and include more sources. With this research, Nicole was able to write a more thorough and detailed paper.

Skill:
Print and Graphic
Features

*Nicole revised her headings to be more specific and to better preview each section's content. The headers keep her research paper more organized.*

dictionaries" (28). As such, storytellers were valuable and honored members of the community.

The oral tradition affected every part of Africans' lives. For these early societies, speech was more than a means of communication. It was power. Janice D. Hamlet explains, "The Africans believed in Nommo, which means the generative power of the spoken word. Nommo was believed necessary to actualize life and give man mastery over things" (27). Speaking allowed these Africans to feel in control over their world. This part of the oral tradition would become especially valuable in the years to come, as many Africans were taken against their will and forced into slavery.

~~Early America~~

~~When the enslaved Africans were brought to America they lost almost everything.Yet, there was one thing they were able to bring with them. Their oral traditions. Folktales were a way to bond and preserve African culture in a new and hostile environment: Told at night, for entertainment as well as instruction, in the traditional African style in which the entire community might be involved in the telling, these stories as performances provided entertainment by which the community could celebrate its identity as a group simply by singing, dancing, and most important, laughing together.~~

Oral Tradition in Early America

When the enslaved Africans were brought to America, they lost almost everything. They lost their homes, their friends and families, and, most importantly, their freedom. Yet, there was one thing they were able to bring with them: their oral traditions. Folktales were a way to bond and to preserve African culture in a new and hostile environment: "Told at night, for entertainment as well as instruction, in the traditional African style in which the entire community might be involved in the telling, these stories as performances provided entertainment by which the community could celebrate its identity as a group simply by singing, dancing, and most important, laughing together" (Abrahams 18).

Thus, storytelling was an escape from the struggles of their daily lives. It's connection to community values brought comfort.

Skill:
Paraphrasing

Storytelling could provide support through hidden messages. Enslaved people could not express themselves openly, instead, they put they're feelings within stories. Such stories often featured animals instead of people. When these stories were overheard slaveholders did not know what they were really talking about. In this way, enslaved people could regain their voices as well as a sense of power (9). The oral tradition had an important practical function, to. An observer might have thought enslaved people were singing "Follow the Drinking Gourd" or "Swing Low, Sweet Chariot" to pass the time, but the lyrics actually concealed coded messages that showed the route to freedom via the Underground Railroad (Hudson 206–207).

**~~Today~~**

~~African American cultural and customs are shared in different ways, but oral traditions continue. Nommo is still alive and well in African American culture, both in the call-and-response nature of African American churches and hip hop culture. (Hamlet 28).~~

The Oral Tradition Continues Today

Today, African American cultural values and customs are shared in many different ways; nevertheless, the lasting effect of the oral tradition is clear. Nommo still plays an active role in African American culture, both in the call-and-response style of African American church services and in hip-hop culture (Hamlet 28). A rap song may seem very different from a traditional folktale, but both share the same heritage.

Storytelling helps us to better understand our past, our present, and our place in the world. Jeff Wallenfeldt says, "It is inevitable, if not essential, that performers take images from the present and wed them to the past, and in that way the past regularly shapes any audience's experience of the present. Storytellers reveal connections between humans—within the world, within a society, within a tribe, within a family" (77). Stories effect us a lot, they form links across generations and across cultures. Every time a story is told, it becomes part of the listener. When enough people hear and share the tale it becomes a part of our experiance. Maybe closeness not entertainment is the goal of storytelling: "Perhaps the real reason

Nicole carefully reread the text to be sure she understood the meaning. Then, she highlighted keywords or phrases in the text that she knew would be important in maintaining the meaning. Nicole rewrote the text in her own words, using the keywords and phrases. By using keywords and phrases when she paraphrased, Nicole was able to maintain the original meaning of the text. As a result, the research paper was a stronger piece of writing and sounded more like Nicole. Most important, she avoided plagiarism.

NOTES

that we tell stories again and again—and endlessly praise our greatest storytellers—is because humans want to be a part of a shared history" (Delistraty). Differences still separate groups of people in today's society, telling stories helps us focus on what we have in comon.

In early Africa, griots told stories. They did this to help their community. The stories helped the community remember where they come from. Over hundreds of years, not much has changed. Authors like Virginia Hamilton and editors like Gates and Tatar have retold traditional stories to help today's audiences understand our shared past and to help shape our future. At bedtime, parents often tell their children old stories not new inventions because those are the stories there parents once told them, a story may change a bit each time its told, however, the way stories help us connect with each other remains the same.

**Works Cited:**

Abrahams, Roger, D. *Afro-American Folktales: Stories from Black Traditions in the New World*. 1995.

Delistraty, Cody C. "The Psychological Comforts of Storytelling." *The Atlantic*, 2 Nov. 2014.

Franklin, John Hope, *From Slavery to Freedom: A History of African Americans*. Knopf. 2000.

Abrahams, Roger, D. *Afro-American Folktales: Stories from Black Traditions in the New World*. Pantheon, 1995.

Delistraty, Cody C. "The Psychological Comforts of Storytelling." *The Atlantic*, 2 Nov. 2014, www.theatlantic.com/health/archive/2014/11/the-psychological-comforts-of-storytelling/381964/.

Franklin, John Hope, and Alfred A. Moss, Jr. *From Slavery to Freedom: A History of African Americans*. Knopf, 2000.

Hamlet, Janice D. "Word! The African American Oral Tradition and its Rhetorical Impact on American Popular Culture." *Black History Bulletin*, vol. 74, no. 1, 2011, pp.27–29.

Skill:
Sources and Citations

Nicole added the publisher to her first citation. She added the website address to the end of the second citation. She also added the second author's name to the third citation. By including all the required information in her citations, Nicole has given proper credit to the sources she used in her research paper. It also lets her readers find these sources on their own.

NOTES

Hudson, J. Blaine. *Encyclopedia of the Underground Railroad.* McFarland, 2006.

Siegel, Robert. "'Annotated African American Folktales' Reclaims Stories Passed Down From Slavery." *All Things Considered*, National Public Radio, 10 Nov. 2017, w w w . n p r . o r g / 2 0 1 7 / 1 1 / 1 0 / 5 6 3 1 1 0 3 7 7 / annotated-african-american-folktales-reclaims-stories-passed-down-from-slavery

Wallenfeldt, Jeff. *Africa to America: From the Middle Passage Through the 1930s.* Rosen, 2010.

# Skill:
# Critiquing Research

## ••• CHECKLIST FOR CRITIQUING RESEARCH

In order to conduct short research projects to answer a question, drawing on several sources, do the following:

- Generate focused questions that are related to your first question in order to guide additional research as needed.

- Gather relevant, or important, information from different print and digital sources.

- Use search terms effectively when looking for information online, such as using unique terms that are specific to your topic (i.e., "daily life in Jamestown, Virginia" rather than just "Jamestown, Virginia").

- Assess your research for accuracy, credibility, and reliability.

To evaluate and use relevant information while conducting short research projects, consider the following questions:

- Does my research come from multiple print and digital sources?

- Have I used search terms effectively when looking for information online?

- Have I generated additional questions to guide any further research I might want to conduct?

- Are there specific terms or phrases in my research question that I can use to adjust my search?

- Can I use "and," "or," or "not" to expand or limit my search?

- Can I use quotation marks to search for exact phrases?

## ⟳ YOUR TURN

Nicole's friend Sherell shared her research plan with Nicole. In the first column of the chart below, they listed some critiques of Sherell's research. Complete the chart by matching Sherell's next steps to each critique.

| | Next Steps |
|---|---|
| A | Sherell should go to a library and ask the librarian to help her find encyclopedias and nonfiction texts to use in her research paper. |
| B | Sherell should check that the sources are well known and respected. She should make sure her sources are from experts in their field, university websites, or well-respected publications. When in doubt, she should ask a teacher. |
| C | After doing some research and taking notes, she should think about additional, focused research questions about her topic that will help her modify her research plan. |
| D | She should make her search terms more specific by using keywords, phrases, and unique terms with quotation marks and words like "and," "or," and "not." |

| Critiques | Next Steps |
|---|---|
| Nicole is unsure about the accuracy, reliability, and credibility of Sherell's sources. | |
| Sherell did a general online search for information and got over a million results. | |
| Sherell only has two sources and both of them are online resources. | |
| Sherell has one general research question, and she is not sure if she will have enough information for a complete informative research paper. | |

**YOUR TURN**

Complete the chart by answering the questions and writing a short summary of what you will do to make changes to your research plan.

| Common Questions or Critiques | My Answers and Next Steps |
|---|---|
| Do you have enough relevant information from a mix of both digital and print sources? | |
| Did you use search terms effectively when conducting online searches? | |
| Are your sources and research accurate, reliable, and credible? | |
| Did you generate additional, focused questions to further and improve your research? | |

# Skill: Paraphrasing

In order to paraphrase, note the following:

- Make sure you understand what the author is saying after reading the text carefully.
- Write down words and phrases that are important to include in a paraphrase to maintain the meaning of the text.
- Look up any words or expressions that are unfamiliar.
- Avoid plagiarism by acknowledging all sources for both paraphrased and quoted material.

To paraphrase texts, consider the following questions:

- Do I understand the meaning of the text?
- Does my paraphrase of the text maintain its original meaning? Have I missed any key points or details?
- Have I avoided plagiarism by acknowledging all my sources for both paraphrased and quoted material?
- Have I noted source information, like the title, author's name, and page number?

Please note that excerpts and passages in the StudySync® library and this workbook are intended as touchstones to generate interest in an author's work. The excerpts and passages do not substitute for the reading of entire texts, and StudySync® strongly recommends that students seek out and purchase the whole literary or informational work in order to experience it as the author intended. Links to online resellers are available in our digital library. In addition, complete works may be ordered through an authorized reseller by filling out and returning to StudySync® the order form enclosed in this workbook.

Reading & Writing
Companion

127

**YOUR TURN**

Read the original text excerpt in the first column of the chart on the following page. In the second column, fill in the keywords from this page that match the text excerpt. Then, in the third column, paraphrase the original text excerpt using the keywords. Remember to cite the author and page number in parentheses. Part of the first row is done for you as an example.

| Keywords |
|---|
| cultural traditions |
| stories |
| African / African American |
| songs |
| storytellers |
| musical |
| passed on |
| again and again |
| old sayings |
| proverbs |
| language |
| word of mouth |
| humans want |
| maintaining |
| tell stories |
| shared history |
| oral tradition |
| Black church |

| Original Text Excerpt | Keywords | Paraphrased Text |
|---|---|---|
| The oral tradition refers to stories, old sayings, songs, proverbs, and other cultural products that have not been written down or recorded. The forms of oral tradition cultures are kept alive by being passed on by word of mouth from one generation to the next.<br><br>*Word! The African American Oral Tradition and Its Rhetorical Impact on American Popular Culture*, Janice D. Hamlet, p. 27 | | To paraphrase: Oral tradition is made up of stories, sayings, and songs or proverbs that have not been written down. These forms of oral tradition are passed down from parents to their children through word of mouth (Hamlet 27). |
| Perhaps the real reason that we tell stories again and again—and endlessly praise our greatest storytellers—is because humans want to be a part of a shared history.<br><br>Delistraty, Cody C. "The Psychological Comforts of Storytelling." *The Atlantic*. 2 Nov. 2014. *The Atlantic Online*. Web. April 2019. | | |
| The musical expressions of African Americans and the Black church have been the most significant forces in maintaining and nurturing the surviving African/African American language cultural traditions.<br><br>*Word! The African American Oral Tradition and Its Rhetorical Impact on American Popular Culture*, Janice D. Hamlet, p. 28 | | |

✏ WRITE

Choose one or two parts of your research paper where information is still in the author's words without quotations or citations or where you can paraphrase the author's words better. Revise those sections using the questions in the checklist.

# Skill:
# Sources and Citations

In order to cite and gather relevant information from multiple print and digital sources, do the following:

- Select and gather information from a variety of print and digital sources using search terms effectively to narrow your search.

- Check that sources are credible and accurate.

- Quote or paraphrase the data you find and cite it to avoid plagiarism, using parenthetical citations, footnotes, or endnotes to credit sources.

- Be sure that facts, details, and other information support your thesis statement.

- Include all sources in a bibliography, following a standard format such as MLA:

  > Halall, Ahmed. *The Pyramids of Ancient Egypt.* Central Publishing, 2016.

  > For a citation, footnote, or endnote, include the author, title, and page number.

To check that sources are gathered and cited correctly, consider the following questions:

- Did I quote or paraphrase the data I found and cite it to avoid plagiarism?

- Have I relied on one source, instead of looking for different points of view on my topic in other sources?

- Did I include all my sources in my bibliography?

- Are my citations formatted correctly using a standard, accepted format?

Copyright © BookheadEd Learning, LLC

## ↻ YOUR TURN

Choose the best answer to each question.

1.  Below is a section from a previous draft of Nicole's research paper. What change should Nicole make to improve the clarity of her citations?

> Collections of folktales are still being compiled and released, both to honor the past and to help shape the future. "To this very day, folktales are being told, altered, retold, and made. A tale naturally changes as it is told by one person to another."

- ○ A.  Add the author's last name in parentheses after the quotation.
- ○ B.  Add the page number in parentheses after the quotation.
- ○ C.  Add the author's last name and the page number in parentheses after the quotation.
- ○ D.  No change needs to be made.

2.  Below is a section from a previous draft of Nicole's works cited page. Which revision best corrects her style errors?

> *The People Could Fly.* Hamilton, Virginia, 1985., Knopf.

- ○ A.  Hamilton, Virginia. *The People Could Fly.* Knopf.
- ○ B.  *The People Could Fly.* Hamilton, Virginia, 1985. Knopf.
- ○ C.  Hamilton, Virginia, *The People Could Fly.* 1985, Knopf.
- ○ D.  Hamilton, Virginia. *The People Could Fly.* Knopf, 1985.

## ✏ WRITE

Use the questions in the checklist section to revise your works cited list. Refer to an MLA style guide or the style guide required by your teacher as needed.

Please note that excerpts and passages in the StudySync® library and this workbook are intended as touchstones to generate interest in an author's work. The excerpts and passages do not substitute for the reading of entire texts, and StudySync® strongly recommends that students seek out and purchase the whole literary or informational work in order to experience it as the author intended. Links to online resellers are available in our digital library. In addition, complete works may be ordered through an authorized reseller by filling out and returning to StudySync® the order form enclosed in this workbook.

Reading & Writing Companion 131

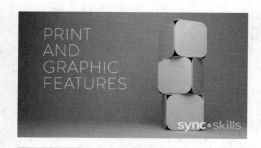

# Skill:
# Print and Graphic Features

## ••• CHECKLIST FOR PRINT AND GRAPHIC FEATURES

First, reread your draft and ask yourself the following questions:

- To what extent would including formatting, graphics, or multimedia be effective in achieving my purpose?
- Which formatting, graphics, or multimedia seem most important in conveying information to the reader?
- How is the addition of the formatting, graphics, or multimedia useful to aiding comprehension?

To include formatting, graphics, and multimedia, using the following questions as a guide:

- How can I use formatting to better organize information? Consider adding:
  - > titles
  - > headings
  - > subheadings
  - > bullets
  - > boldface and italicized terms

- How can I use graphics to better convey information? Consider adding:
  - > charts
  - > graphs
  - > tables
  - > timelines
  - > diagrams
  - > figures and statistics
  - > images with captions

- How can I use multimedia to add interest and variety? Consider adding a combination of:
  - > photographs
  - > art
  - > audio
  - > video

## ↻ YOUR TURN

Choose the best answer to each question.

1. Nicole has decided to include a timeline in a draft of a section of her paper titled "Today." Read the section below. How does including a timeline make this section of her paper more effective?

---

### Today

African American cultural and customs are shared in different ways, but oral traditions continue. Nommo still plays an active role in African American culture, both in the call-and-response style of African American church services and in hip-hop culture (Hamlet 28). A rap song may seem very different from a traditional folktale, but both share the same heritage.

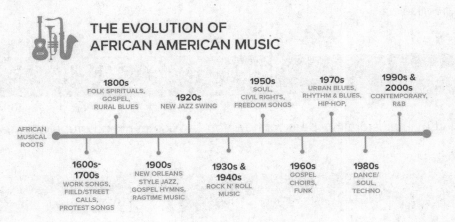

**THE EVOLUTION OF AFRICAN AMERICAN MUSIC**

Jeff Wallenfeldt says, "It is inevitable, if not essential, that performers take images from the present and wed them to the past, and in that way the past regularly shapes any audience's experience of the present. Storytellers reveal connections between humans—within the world, within a society, within a tribe, within a family" (77). Stories affect us a lot; they form links across generations and across cultures.

---

○ A. The timeline helps readers see the progression of the African American oral tradition, including culture and music.

○ B. The timeline helps Nicole organize her information more effectively.

○ C. The timeline is an example of multimedia used to add variety and interest to her research paper.

○ D. The timeline is a print feature that will highlight a specific section of the text.

Please note that excerpts and passages in the StudySync® library and this workbook are intended as touchstones to generate interest in an author's work. The excerpts and passages do not substitute for the reading of entire texts, and StudySync® strongly recommends that students seek out and purchase the whole literary or informational work in order to experience it as the author intended. Links to online resellers are available in our digital library. In addition, complete works may be ordered through an authorized reseller by filling out and returning to StudySync® the order form enclosed in this workbook.

Reading & Writing Companion    133

2. Nicole wants to revise the header "Today" to better reflect the content of this section from a draft of her paper. Reread the first few sentences of the section and then select the best revision.

---

Today

African American culture and customs are shared in different ways, but oral traditions continue. Nommo still plays an active role in African American culture, both in the call-and-response style of African American church services and in hip-hop culture (Hamlet 28). A rap song may seem very different from a traditional folktale, but both share the same heritage.

---

○ A. African American Values and Customs

○ B. The Oral Tradition Continues Today

○ C. Call and Response

○ D. Rap and Folktales

## ↻ YOUR TURN

Complete the chart by brainstorming ideas for how you can use print and graphic features to improve your research paper.

| Print and Graphic Feature or Multimedia | My Ideas and Changes |
| --- | --- |
| How can I use formatting to better organize information? | |
| How can I use graphics to better convey information? | |
| How can I use multimedia to add interest and variety? | |

# Research Writing Process: Revise

| PLAN | DRAFT | REVISE | EDIT AND PUBLISH |
|------|-------|--------|------------------|

You have written a draft of your informative research paper. You have also received input from your peers about how to improve it. Now you are going to revise your draft.

## ⬅ REVISION GUIDE

Examine your draft to find areas for revision. Keep in mind your purpose and audience as you revise for clarity, development, organization, and style. Use the guide below to help you review:

| Review | Revise | Example |
|--------|--------|---------|
| **Clarity** | | |
| Label each term that is specific to the topic you've researched. Annotate any places where the meaning of the term is unclear. | Add description to clarify the meaning of any unfamiliar terms. | Griots, or storytellers, collected songs and stories as a way of protecting and sharing cultural values and customs. |
| **Development** | | |
| Identify key ideas in your research paper. Annotate places where additional description or information could help develop your ideas. | Make sure you have a strong main idea in each paragraph, and add description or information to develop your ideas. | Nommo is still alive and well in African American culture, both in the call-and-response nature of African American churches and hip hop culture. (Hamlet 28). A rap song may seem very different from a traditional folktale, but both share the same heritage. |

| Review | Revise | Example |
|---|---|---|
| **Organization** | | |
| Review your body paragraphs. Identify and annotate any sentences that don't flow in a clear and logical way. | Rewrite the sentences so they appear in a clear and logical order, starting with a strong transition or topic sentence. Make sure to include a transition between body paragraphs. | Janice D. Hamlet explains, "The Africans believed in Nommo, which means the generative power of the spoken word. Nommo was believed necessary to actualize life and give man mastery over things" (27). Speaking allowed these Africans to feel in control over their world. This part of the oral tradition would become especially valuable in the years to come, as many Africans were taken against their will and forced into slavery. |
| **Style: Word Choice** | | |
| Identify weak or repetitive words or phrases that do not clearly express your ideas to the reader. | Replace weak and repetitive words and phrases with more descriptive ones that better convey your ideas. | Gates and his co-editor, Maria Tatar, are two ~~people~~ links in a very long chain of storytellers who have worked to keep the oral tradition of storytelling alive. |
| **Style: Sentence Variety** | | |
| Read your essay aloud. Annotate places where you have too many long or short sentences in a row. | Revise short sentences by linking them together. Shorten longer sentences for clarity of emphasis. | In early Africa, griots told stories.~~They did this~~ to help their community.~~The stories helped the community~~ remember where they came from. Over hundreds of years, not much has changed. |

✏ WRITE

Use the guide above, as well as your peer reviews, to help you evaluate your informative research paper to determine areas that should be revised.

# Grammar: Participial Phrases

## Participial Phrase

A participle is a verb form that acts as an adjective to modify a noun or pronoun. A participle can be present or past. A present participle ends in *-ing*. A past participle usually ends in *-ed* but includes irregular forms as well, such as *chosen* and *sung*.

A participial phrase begins with a present or past participle and includes other words that complete its meaning. Like a participle, a participial phrase acts as an adjective. The phrase can appear before or after the noun or pronoun it modifies. Be sure to place the phrase as close as possible to the modified word in order to make the meaning of the sentence clear..

| Correct | Incorrect |
|---|---|
| Growling furiously, the bear clawed at the bars of its cage. | The bear clawed, growling furiously, at the bars of its cage. |
| The insects mounted in this frame are part of a much larger collection. | The insects are part of a much larger collection mounted in this frame. |

Follow these punctuation rules when using participial phrases:

| Rule | Text |
|---|---|
| Use a comma to set off a participial phrase that begins a sentence. | **Chastened by the experience,** Chang-bo was more careful about what he said outside the family, but his thoughts were running wild.<br><br>Nothing to Envy: Ordinary Lives in North Korea |
| Use commas to set off a participial phrase that is not essential to the meaning of the sentence. | The women, **wearing faded house dresses and sweaters,** came shortly after their menfolk.<br><br>The Lottery |
| No punctuation is necessary when the phrase is not at the beginning of the sentence and is essential to the meaning of the sentence. | He issued an edict **abolishing gladiatorial combat** in a.d. 323.<br><br>Gladiator |

## ⟳ YOUR TURN

1.  How should this sentence be changed?

    > Life fills a forest springing from every spot.

    ○  A.  Place the phrase **springing from every spot** in the beginning of the sentence, and put a comma after the word **spot**.

    ○  B.  Insert a comma after the word **springing**.

    ○  C.  Insert a comma after the word **Life**.

    ○  D.  No change needs to be made to this sentence.

2.  How should this sentence be changed?

    > The radio, tuned to my favorite station, was bothering my mother.

    ○  A.  Delete the comma after the word **radio**.

    ○  B.  Delete the comma after the word **station**.

    ○  C.  Delete both commas after the words **radio** and **station**.

    ○  D.  No change needs to be made to this sentence.

3.  How should this sentence be changed?

    > Smoke, billowing from the chimneys, darkened the sky.

    ○  A.  Delete the comma after the word **Smoke**.

    ○  B.  Delete the comma after the word **chimneys**.

    ○  C.  Delete the commas after the word **Smoke** and after the word **chimneys**.

    ○  D.  No change needs to be made to this sentence.

4.  How should this sentence be changed?

    > Erik, dreaming of fame sits at the piano.

    ○  A.  Delete the comma after the word **Erik**.

    ○  B.  Insert a comma after the word **fame**.

    ○  C.  Insert a comma after the word **dreaming**.

    ○  D.  No change needs to be made to this sentence.

# Grammar: Gerunds and Gerund Phrases

A gerund is a verb form that ends in *-ing* and acts as a noun. A gerund phrase includes the gerund and all the other words that complete its meaning. A gerund phrase is used as a noun phrase in a sentence. That means that a gerund phrase can be the subject of the sentence, the direct object of a verb, and the object of a preposition.

| Text | Explanation |
|---|---|
| **Crushing certain plants** could add up infinitesimally.<br><br>A Sound of Thunder | The gerund phrase *crushing certain plants* is the subject of this sentence. |
| "He started **digging ditches and stuff**, and the next thing you knew, he was sitting by his own swimming pool."<br><br>Born Worker | The gerund phrase *digging ditches and stuff* is the direct object of the verb *started*. (The word *sitting* is not a gerund. It is part of a verb.) |
| A year later, he felt guilty for **letting his group down**.<br><br>A Role to Play | The gerund phrase *letting his group down* is the object of the preposition *for*. |

## ♻ YOUR TURN

1. Which sentence contains a gerund phrase?

   ○ A. Collecting stamps is a fun hobby to have.
   ○ B. Joanne is watching her little brother play.
   ○ C. Are you happy to have a role in the play?
   ○ D. None of the above

2. Which sentence contains a gerund phrase?

   ○ A. Watch where you step!
   ○ B. Coming through the woods, Jack lost his house keys.
   ○ C. Marla enjoys making pizza for the family.
   ○ D. None of the above

3. Which sentence contains a gerund phrase?

   ○ A. Zeke tiptoed into the house softly, scaring the cat.
   ○ B. Jason is going on a visit to his uncle's tree farm.
   ○ C. The red kangaroo hopped quickly through the field.
   ○ D. None of the above

4. Which sentence contains a gerund phrase?

   ○ A. Michael decided to learn how to weave rugs.
   ○ B. You can get into trouble by jumping to conclusions.
   ○ C. The cat was spitting mad.
   ○ D. None of the above

# Grammar: Infinitive Phrases

**Infinitive Phrases**

An infinitive phrase contains an infinitive (such as *to throw*) and other words that complete its meaning. If other words are not present, then the sentence simply contains an infinitive, not an infinitive phrase.

The word *to* is a preposition when it is followed by a noun or pronoun as an object of the preposition. The word *to* used before the base form of a verb is part of the infinitive form of the verb. It is not a preposition.

| Infinitive | Infinitive Phrase |
|---|---|
| Carlos loves **to run**. | Carlos loves **to run marathons**. |
| Grandma does not want **to cook**. | Grandma does not want **to cook liver and onions tonight**. |

Use these guidelines when using infinitive phrases:

| Guideline | Text |
|---|---|
| An infinitive phrase may include a direct object. | Otto shook the ashes out of his pipe and squatted down **to count the rattles**.<br><br>My Antonia |
| An infinitive phrase may include an adverb. | If children are aware that their parents can see everything they do, they are more likely **to behave appropriately**.<br><br>The Dangers of Social Media |
| An infinitive phrase may include a prepositional phrase. | Encarnación acted out how boys learned **to fish in the Philippines**.<br><br>Barrio Boy |

Infinitive phrases, like infinitives, can function as nouns, adjectives, or adverbs. They often function as nouns and serve as the subject, direct object, or predicate noun in a sentence.

## ↻ YOUR TURN

1. How should this sentence be changed to include an infinitive phrase?

> I clambered up the ladder.

- ○ A. Add *to look* after *ladder.*
- ○ B. Add *to the building's roof* after *ladder.*
- ○ C. Add *to see around the building* after *ladder.*
- ○ D. No change needs to be made to this sentence.

2. How should this sentence be changed to include an infinitive phrase?

> To run around the racetrack is exhausting!

- ○ A. Add *to the finish line* after *racetrack.*
- ○ B. Add *after school* after *racetrack.*
- ○ C. Remove *around the racetrack* from the sentence.
- ○ D. No change needs to be made to this sentence.

3. How should this sentence be changed to include an infinitive phrase?

> He wanted to learn.

- ○ A. Add *an eager student,* before *he.*
- ○ B. Add *the rules of badminton* after *learn.*
- ○ C. Remove the word *to.*
- ○ D. No change needs to be made to this sentence.

4. How should this sentence be changed to include an infinitive phrase?

> Dig in a sandbox is one of the most enjoyable experiences of childhood.

- ○ A. Add *to* before *dig.*
- ○ B. Add *to* before *a sandbox.*
- ○ C. Add *furiously* after *dig.*
- ○ D. No change needs to be made to this sentence.

# Research Writing Process: Edit and Publish

| PLAN | DRAFT | REVISE | EDIT AND PUBLISH |

You have revised your research paper based on your peer feedback and your own examination.

Now, it is time to edit your research paper. When you revised, you focused on the content of your research paper. You probably critiqued your sources and reviewed your use of quotations, paraphrasing, and sources. When you edit, you focus on the mechanics of your research paper, paying close attention to things like grammar and punctuation.

**Use the checklist below to guide you as you edit:**

☐ Have I used a variety of phrases in my writing, including

- participial phrases?

- gerund phrases?

- infinitive phrases?

☐ Do I have any sentence fragments or run-on sentences?

☐ Have I spelled everything correctly?

**Notice some edits Nicole has made:**

- Changed her phrasing to include a participial phrase.

- Included several infinitive phrases.

- Broke up a run-on sentence into two separate sentences.

Please note that excerpts and passages in the StudySync® library and this workbook are intended as touchstones to generate interest in an author's work. The excerpts and passages do not substitute for the reading of entire texts, and StudySync® strongly recommends that students seek out and purchase the whole literary or informational work in order to experience it as the author intended. Links to online resellers are available in our digital library. In addition, complete works may be ordered through an authorized reseller by filling out and returning to StudySync® the order form enclosed in this workbook.

Reading & Writing Companion  **143**

In early Africa, griots told stories to help their community remember where they came from. Over hundreds of years, not much has changed. Authors and storytellers as well as editors like Gates and Tatar have retold traditional stories to help today's audiences understand our shared past and to help shape our future. At bedtime, parents ~~often tell~~ can often be found telling their children old stories, not new inventions, because those are the stories their parents once told them~~., a~~ A story may change a bit each time it's told; however, the way stories help us connect with each other remains the same.

## ✏ WRITE

Use the questions on the previous page, as well as your peer reviews, to help you evaluate your research paper to determine areas that need editing. Then edit your research paper to correct those errors.

Once you have made all your corrections, you are ready to publish your work. You can distribute your writing to family and friends, hang it on a bulletin board, or post it on your blog. If you publish online, share the link with your family, friends, and classmates.

# The Legendary Storyteller

INFORMATIONAL TEXT

## Introduction

Most readers are likely already familiar with many of Aesop's fables. Parents all over the world have been telling these stories to their children for thousands of years. Despite being possibly the world's best-known storyteller, Aesop remains a mystery. Aesop himself had not been mentioned in writing until a hundred years after his death. The story of his life has been pieced together from numerous, and often conflicting, stories. Some historians question if he ever existed at all.

## V VOCABULARY

**alias**

a name someone uses instead of his or her real name

**frame**

to falsely make a person look guilty of a crime

**counsel**

an advisor; someone who gives advice

**definitive**

absolute and without a doubt

**unappreciative**

not thankful

NOTES

## ≡ READ

1   Aesop wrote stories like "The Tortoise and the Hare" and "The Boy Who Cried Wolf." His stories have been told many times in many languages. Phrases like "sour grapes" and "a bird in the hand is worth two in the bush" came from his stories. We know little about Aesop. Aesop never wrote down his tales. We do not know if Aesop made up these stories or just collected them. Some historians think Aesop was not real. These historians think that multiple writers simply took up the **alias** "Aesop." All of our knowledge of Aesop has been passed down in stories, just like his fables.

2   Aesop's most famous fable has a tortoise beat a hare. Many of his stories feature weak and poor heroes. This may be due to how he grew up. Most historians agree that Aesop was born into slavery sometime around 620 B.C.E. We are not sure where Aesop was from. He might have been born on an island near Turkey. He might have been Phrygian. Some historians think he came from Africa. Aesop's stories of animals and tricksters carry on the traditions of African folklore.

3   Aesop was very clever. His intelligence stood out so much that the slaveholder set him free. Aesop traveled and told his stories. He also became involved in politics. He used stories to convince King Croesus of Lydia to lower taxes. Aesop's wisdom impressed King Croesus. He gave Aesop a job as a **counsel** on his court. Aesop also made enemies. King Croesus asked Aesop to give gold to the people of Delphi. There was a mix-up over how much gold each person should receive. The Delphians argued. Aesop decided they were being **unappreciative**. Aesop made up his mind to take the gold back to King Croesus. The angry Delphians decided to **frame** Aesop. The Delphians hid a golden bowl from the Temple of Apollo among Aesop's things. Then the Delphians accused Aesop of stealing the bowl. The Delphians threw Aesop off the nearby cliffs. This was the punishment for thieves in Delphi.

4   Aesop's life was almost as fantastic as his tales themselves. His stories have touched the lives of people all over the world, but historians have not come up with any **definitive** proof that Aesop was a real person. It is fitting that the master storyteller may be a myth himself.

# First Read

Read the text. After you read, answer the Think Questions below.

## ☁ THINK QUESTIONS

1. What is Aesop most famous for?

   _____

   _____.

2. Where did Aesop come from?

   _____

   _____.

3. What did the Delphians accuse Aesop of doing?

   _____

   _____.

4. Use context to confirm the meaning of the word *frame* as it is used in "The Legendary Storyteller." Write your definition of *frame* here.

   _____

   _____.

5. What is another way to say that evidence is *definitive*?

   _____

   _____.

 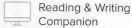 

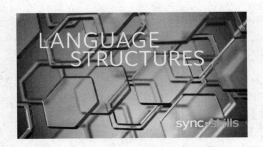

# Skill:
# Language Structures

## ★ DEFINE

In every language, there are rules that tell how to **structure** sentences. These rules define the correct order of words. In the English language, for example, a **basic** structure for sentences is subject, verb, and object. Some sentences have more **complicated** structures.

You will encounter both basic and complicated **language structures** in the classroom materials you read. Being familiar with language structures will help you better understand the text.

## ••• CHECKLIST FOR LANGUAGE STRUCTURES

To improve your comprehension of language structures, do the following:

✓ Monitor your understanding.

- Ask yourself: Why do I not understand this sentence? Is it because I do not understand some of the words? Or is it because I do not understand the way the words are ordered in the sentence?

✓ Pay attention to verbs followed by prepositions.

- A **verb** names an action.

  > Example: I **sit** on my chair.

  > This tells the reader what the subject of the sentence is doing (sitting).

- A **preposition** defines the relationship between two or more nouns or verbs in a sentence.

  > Example: I sit **on** my chair.

  > This tells the reader where the subject is doing the action (on a chair).

Please note that excerpts and passages in the StudySync® library and this workbook are intended as touchstones to generate interest in an author's work. The excerpts and passages do not substitute for the reading of entire texts, and StudySync® strongly recommends that students seek out and purchase the whole literary or informational work in order to experience it as the author intended. Links to online resellers are available in our digital library. In addition, complete works may be ordered through an authorized reseller by filling out and returning to StudySync® the order form enclosed in this workbook.

Reading & Writing Companion    **149**

- Sometimes the preposition comes directly after the verb, but it can also be separated by another word.

  > Example: I **took** it **to** school with me.

- Sometimes the preposition changes the meaning of the verb. This is called a **phrasal verb.**

  > Example: The teacher liked to **call on** the students in the front of the class.

  > The phrasal verb *call on* means "to select someone to share information."

✓ Break down the sentence into its parts.

- Ask yourself: What words make up the verbs in this sentence? Is the verb followed by a preposition? How does this affect the meaning of the sentence?

## ↻ YOUR TURN

Notice the verb + preposition pairs in the sentences. Write the letter for each sentence in the correct category.

| | Verb + Preposition Pairs |
|---|---|
| A | His intelligence stood out so much that the slaveholder set him free. |
| B | Some historians think he came from Africa. |
| C | Aesop's stories of animals and tricksters carry on the traditions of African folklore. |
| D | He might have been born on an island near Turkey. |

| Phrasal Verb | Non-Phrasal Verb |
|---|---|
| | |
| | |

Reading & Writing Companion

# Skill:
# Visual and Contextual Support

## ★ DEFINE

**Visual support** is an image or an object that helps you understand a text. **Contextual support** is a **feature** that helps you understand a text. By using visual and contextual supports, you can develop your vocabulary so you can better understand a variety of texts.

First, preview the text to identify any visual supports. These might include illustrations, graphics, charts, or other objects in a text. Then, identify any contextual supports. Examples of contextual supports are titles, heads, captions, and boldface terms. Write down your **observations**.

Then, write down what those visual and contextual supports tell you about the meaning of the text. Note any new vocabulary that you see in those supports. Ask your peers and your teacher to confirm your understanding of the text.

## ••• CHECKLIST FOR VISUAL AND CONTEXTUAL SUPPORT

To use visual and contextual support to understand texts, do the following:

✓ Preview the text. Read the title, headers, and other features. Look at any images and graphics.

✓ Write down the visual and contextual supports in the text.

✓ Write down what those supports tell you about the text.

✓ Note any new vocabulary that you see in those supports.

✓ Confirm your observations with your peers and teacher.

✓ Create an illustration for the reading and write a descriptive caption.

**YOUR TURN**

Write the letter for each example of Visual and Contextual Supports into the correct columns.

| Support from the Article | |
|---|---|
| **A** | a map that shows the possible locations of Aesop's birth |
| **B** | a caption describing an illustration for "The Tortoise and the Hare" |
| **C** | a heading at that says: "Aesop and the Delphians" |
| **D** | an illustration of the bowl that the Delphians hid among Aesop's things |

| Visual | Contextual |
|---|---|
|  |  |
|  |  |

# The Legendary Storyteller

# Close Read

---

✏ **WRITE**

INFORMATIVE: How did Aesop's life reflect his fables? Write a short paragraph in which you explain how Aesop's life is similar to his stories. Use details from the text and your background knowledge of fables. Be sure to include appropriate topic vocabulary in your writing. Pay attention to spelling rules as you write.

**Use the checklist below to guide you as you write.**

☐  What is the main theme in many of Aesop's fables?

☐  What were the major events in Aesop's life?

☐  How is Aesop's life similar to Aesop's fables?

**Use the sentence frames to organize and write your informational paragraph.**

Many of Aesop's fables are about _____.

The _____ are really _____.

They use their _____ to succeed.

Aesop was a _____.

He used his _____ to _____.

He became _____.

Aesop's life is like his stories. He was an _____,

but he _____.

---

# The Worried Armadillo

FICTION

## Introduction

The pressures of school, work, family, and friends can sometimes seem overwhelming. While it's important to care about your responsibilities, too much stress can do more harm than good. In this modern fable, an armadillo

## ⓥ VOCABULARY

**mural**
an artistic painting on a wall

**detergent**
a cleaning liquid

**commemorate**
to honor a memory

**kaleidoscope**
a toy containing mirrors and colored glass that creates colorful patterns

**catastrophe**
a disaster

## ≡ READ

NOTES

1   Once there was an armadillo. Like all armadillos, he had armor protecting his body. Whenever he felt in danger, he could curl up into a ball and nothing could hurt him. His armor was his pride and joy.

2   The armadillo was also an artist. He was known all over the town for his talent, so the mayor asked him to paint a black-and-white **mural** to **commemorate** the town's growth. When he began painting, the armadillo slipped and fell off his ladder. His shell protected him from harm, but paint spattered all over him.

3   The armadillo wailed over this **catastrophe**. Covered in white and black paint, he looked like a soccer ball. He thought that bored children would kick him. A coyote heard his cries of despair. Once she realized he wasn't a soccer ball, she offered him a solution. She had a special **detergent** that could remove stains. She had used it before to clean ink from her fur. The coyote offered to use some of the leftover detergent to fix the armadillo's armor.

NOTES

4   The coyote filled a tub with water and poured in a liquid from a bottle. The water shifted through a **kaleidoscope** of colors before finally settling on a shade of bright green. The armadillo removed his armor and put it in the tub. The coyote told the armadillo that it would take three days for the detergent to take effect. The armadillo asked if she was pulling his leg. Three days seemed too long to be without his precious armor.

5   With a long face, the armadillo returned to his home. Over the next three days, he was unable to sleep a wink. He'd wonder what would happen if he got into an accident or worse—what would happen if the treatment didn't work? He became unhealthy. He forgot to eat and became rail-thin. When the third day finally came, the armadillo rushed to the coyote's home.

6   The coyote, who never minced words, told the armadillo that he looked terrible. The armadillo explained the sleepless nights and missed meals. Then he asked to see his armor. The coyote retrieved the armor. It was spotless. Excited, the armadillo tried to slide it onto his body, but he had become so thin that the armor fell off. The coyote scolded him for not taking care of himself. She said, "My friend, there's nothing wrong with showing concern, but look at yourself! Worrying didn't fix your problems. It just made things worse."

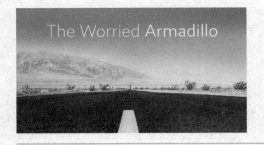

# First Read

Read the story. After you read, answer the Think Questions below.

## ☁ THINK QUESTIONS

1. What bad thing happened to the armadillo at the start of the fable?

_____

_____

2. How does the coyote offer to help the armadillo?

_____

_____

3. What problem does the armadillo have at the end of the fable?

_____

_____

4. Use context to confirm the meaning of the word *detergent* as it is used in "The Worried Armadillo." Write your definition of *detergent* here.

_____

_____

5. What is another way to say that the party was a *catastrophe*?

_____

_____

Please note that excerpts and passages in the StudySync® library and this workbook are intended as touchstones to generate interest in an author's work. The excerpts and passages do not substitute for the reading of entire texts, and StudySync® strongly recommends that students seek out and purchase the whole literary or informational work in order to experience it as the author intended. Links to online resellers are available in our digital library. In addition, complete works may be ordered through an authorized reseller by filling out and returning to StudySync® the order form enclosed in this workbook.

Reading & Writing Companion 157

# Skill: Analyzing Expressions

## ★ DEFINE

When you read, you may find English expressions that you do not know. An **expression** is a group of words that communicates an idea. Two types of expressions are **idioms** and **sayings**. They can be difficult to understand because the meanings of the words are different from their **literal**, or usual, meanings.

An **idiom** is an expression that is commonly known among a group of people. For example: "It's raining cats and dogs" means it is raining heavily. **Sayings** are short expressions that contain advice or wisdom. For instance: "Don't count your chickens before they hatch" means do not plan on something good happening before it happens. Neither expression is about actual animals.

## ••• CHECKLIST FOR ANALYZING EXPRESSIONS

To determine the meaning of an expression, remember the following:

✓ If you find a confusing group of words, it may be an expression. The meaning of words in expressions may not be their literal meaning.

- Ask yourself: Is this confusing because the words are new? Or because the words do not make sense together?

✓ Determining the overall meaning may require that you use one or more of the following:

- context clues

- a dictionary or other resource

- teacher or peer support

✓ Highlight important information before and after the expression to look for clues.

**YOUR TURN**

Read the following excerpt from paragraph 4 of the story. Then, complete the multiple-choice questions below.

---

from "The Worried Armadillo"

The coyote filled a tub with water and poured in a liquid from a bottle. The water shifted through a kaleidoscope of colors before finally settling on a shade of bright green. The armadillo removed his armor and put it in the tub. The coyote told the armadillo that it would take three days for the detergent to take effect. The armadillo asked if she was pulling his leg. Three days seemed too long to be without his precious armor.

---

1. What does "if she was pulling his leg" mean in this story?

   ○ A. if the coyote was holding the armadillo's leg
   ○ B. if the coyote was joking with the armadillo
   ○ C. if the coyote was upset with the armadillo
   ○ D. if the coyote was going to help the armadillo

2. Which context clue helped you determine the meaning of the expression?

   ○ A. "The coyote filled a tub with water and poured in a liquid from a bottle."
   ○ B. "The armadillo removed his armor and put it in the tub."
   ○ C. "three days for the detergent to take effect"
   ○ D. "Three days seemed too long to be without his precious armor."

Please note that excerpts and passages in the StudySync® library and this workbook are intended as touchstones to generate interest in an author's work. The excerpts and passages do not substitute for the reading of entire texts, and StudySync® strongly recommends that students seek out and purchase the whole literary or informational work in order to experience it as the author intended. Links to online resellers are available in our digital library. In addition, complete works may be ordered through an authorized reseller by filling out and returning to StudySync® the order form enclosed in this workbook.

Reading & Writing Companion    **159**

# Skill: Drawing Inferences and Conclusions

 **DEFINE**

Making **inferences** means connecting your experiences with what you read. Authors do not always tell readers directly everything that takes place in a story or text. You need to use clues to infer, or make a guess, about what is happening. To make an inference, first find facts, details, and examples in the text. Then think about what you already know. Combine the **text evidence** with your **background knowledge** to draw a **conclusion** about what the author is trying to communicate.

Making inferences and drawing conclusions can help you better understand what you are reading. It may also help you search for and find the author's message in the text.

## ••• CHECKLIST FOR DRAWING INFERENCES AND CONCLUSIONS

In order to make inferences and draw conclusions, do the following:

✓ Look for information that is missing from the text or that is not directly stated.

- Ask yourself: What is confusing? What is missing?

✓ Think about what you already know about the topic.

- Ask yourself: Have I had a similar experience in my life? Have I learned about this subject in another class?

✓ Combine clues from the text with prior knowledge to make an inference and draw a conclusion.

- Think: I can conclude _____
  because the text says _____
  and I know that _____.

✓ Use text evidence to support your inference and make sure that it is valid.

## ↻ YOUR TURN

Read the following excerpt from paragraphs 1 and 2 of the story. Then, complete the multiple-choice questions below.

---

from "The Worried Armadillo"

Once there was an armadillo. Like all armadillos, he had armor protecting his body. Whenever he felt in danger, he could curl up into a ball and nothing could hurt him. His armor was his pride and joy.

The armadillo was also an artist. He was known all over the town for his talent, so the mayor asked him to paint a black-and-white mural to commemorate the town's growth. When he began painting, the armadillo slipped and fell off his ladder. His shell protected him from harm, but paint spattered all over him.

---

1. At the beginning of the excerpt, the armadillo:

   ○ A. wants to curl up into a ball.

   ○ B. feels like he is in danger.

   ○ C. loves his armor.

   ○ D. feels like he does not need his armor.

2. A detail that best supports this conclusion is:

   ○ A. "like all armadillos"

   ○ B. "he could curl up"

   ○ C. "nothing could hurt him"

   ○ D. "His armor was his pride and joy."

3. Details at the beginning of paragraph 2 tell that the armadillo is a:

   ○ A. photographer.

   ○ B. friend of the mayor.

   ○ C. very good painter.

   ○ D. historian.

4. A detail that best supports this conclusion is:

   ○ A. "The armadillo was also an artist."

   ○ B. "known all over town for his talent"

   ○ C. "a black-and-white mural"

   ○ D. "the town's growth"

Please note that excerpts and passages in the StudySync® library and this workbook are intended as touchstones to generate interest in an author's work. The excerpts and passages do not substitute for the reading of entire texts, and StudySync® strongly recommends that students seek out and purchase the whole literary or informational work in order to experience it as the author intended. Links to online resellers are available in our digital library. In addition, complete works may be ordered through an authorized reseller by filling out and returning to StudySync® the order form enclosed in this workbook.

Reading & Writing Companion    161

# Close Read

---

 **WRITE**

NARRATIVE: Rewrite the fable so that it teaches a new moral. Use characters, events, and details from the original text. Pay attention to negatives and contractions as you write.

**Use the checklist below to guide you as you write.**

☐ Which characters are involved?

☐ What is a problem that happens in the fable?

☐ What is the moral that the reader learns?

**Use the sentence frames to organize and write your narrative.**

Once, there was an armadillo _____.

A coyote heard him crying and _____.

The coyote _____.

But the armadillo _____.

The coyote said, "If you take your armor now, _____

_____."

The coyote said, "Remember that if you are going to do a job well, _____

_____."